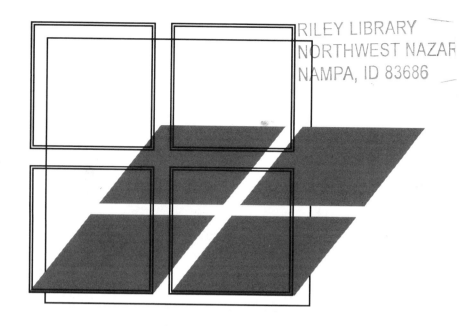

DATE DUE

Literacy Assessment

A Handbook of Instruments

Edited by Lynn K. Rhodes

HEINEMANN
Portsmouth, NH

Heinemann
A division of Reed Elsevier Inc.
361 Hanover Street
Portsmouth, NH 03801-3912

Offices and agents throughout the world

© 1993 by Heinemann Educational Books, Inc.

Library of Congress Cataloging-in-Publication Data

Literacy assessment: a handbook of instruments/edited by Lynn K.
  Rhodes.
     p. cm.
    Includes bibliographical references.
    ISBN 0-435-08759-2
    1. Reading—Ability testing—Handbooks, manuals, etc.   2. Language
arts (Elementary)—Handbooks, manuals, etc.   3. Language experience
approach in education—Handbooks, manuals, etc.   I. Rhodes, Lynn
Knebel.
LB1050.46.L58   1993
428.4'076—dc20   92–1619
                                                                           CIP

Printed in the United States of America on acid free paper

96 97   7 6 5

Contents

5. Program Placement 163

6. Assessing the Teaching of Literacy 169

7. The Assessment and Evaluation of Literacy 179

Introduction

In *Windows Into Literacy: Assessing Learners K-8*, Nancy Shanklin and I defined assessment as the process of carefully collecting or recording and analyzing students' literacy products and processes in order to inform instruction. This handbook contains instruments that we—and many teachers we know—have found useful in gathering literacy assessment data. These instruments are either discussed in *Windows Into Literacy* or are related to other instruments included in that book.

Assessment instruments must be directly linked to a teacher's instruction, instructional goals, and assessment questions if they are to be helpful. Although the instruments in this book may be photocopied by teachers for use in assessment, we hope that the teachers who use them will review them carefully and revise them as necessary in order to answer their own particular assessment questions about their students' literacy. Teachers make choices and adapt the curriculum in order to meet their students' needs, and they should approach these assessment instruments in the same way.

Reading

Interviews and Attitude Surveys

Reading Survey
Reading Interview
Content Reading Interview
Denver Reading Attitude Survey
Elementary Reading Attitude Survey
An Inventory of Classroom Reading Use

Interviews and attitude surveys are most often in an open-ended format or a Lickert scale format. Examples of each kind are included here.

The *Reading Survey* is one that Nancie Atwell used with her middle school students in Boothbay Harbor, Maine. Although students' written responses to the questions enable a teacher to understand students' perceptions of reading and reading instruction (like the *Reading Interview* that follows), the survey focuses on students' reading habits, interests, and attitudes toward reading. The open-ended format provides rich information when students fully respond to it. If a student does not fully respond, it is helpful to follow up with an oral interview. When using this survey, consider revisions that will elicit information that is of importance to you.

The *Reading Interview* is intended to be an oral interview. It was developed by Carolyn Burke of Indiana University and is included in *Reading Miscue Inventory: Alternative Procedures* (Goodman, Watson & Burke, 1987). In addition to tapping students' attitudes about themselves as readers, the interview also provides information about students' perceptions of reading and reading instruction.

The scoring taxonomy that accompanies the interview, Reading Interview: Coding Directions, developed by Burke, Curt Dudley-Marling and Lynn Rhodes, is designed to be used by teachers who want to aggregate the information they collect from students. It may also be used to help teachers understand the wide variety of possible responses, particularly when their students provide only a narrow range of responses.

The *Content Reading Interview* was adapted from Vacca and Vacca (1989) to uncover students' perceptions of reading in content areas such as science and social studies. If you are a reading teacher working with students who are struggling in content area classes taken with other teachers, this interview can be especially helpful in providing insights about the nature of the struggle.

The *Denver Reading Attitude Survey* has a Lickert scale format. It was developed by W. Alan Davis and Lynn K. Rhodes and administered as part of a research project conducted by ten University of Colorado at Denver researchers in forty fourth- and fifth-grade classrooms and has been revised on the basis of the research data. The survey is provided in both English and Spanish.

The *Elementary Reading Attitude Survey* (McKenna & Kear, 1990) also has a Lickert scale format. It is child-friendly, using Garfield figures (from broadly smiling to frowning) to represent students' feelings about various aspects of reading. Grades 1-6 norm-referenced data for the scale may be found in McKenna and Kear (1990). The scale assesses both recreational and academic reading attitudes. Teachers need to consider how well each "academic reading" item reflects their beliefs about age-appropriateness and the nature of academic reading, since these items reflect a traditional reading curriculum. Information about norms and validity may also be found in the original publication.

An Inventory of Classroom Reading Use was designed by a Denver group, CAWLs (Coordinators/Consultants Applying Whole Language), in order to assist teachers in examining students' progress toward making reading an important part of their lives by exploring how and how much students use reading in their lives.

Besides indicating the degree to which each student uses reading in the particular way suggested by each item, the inventory can also indicate whether this use is initiated by the teacher, by the student, or both. This allows the teacher to assess his or her own initiation of the use of reading for a variety of purposes in the classroom and whether the student has independently initiated use of reading for particular purposes. Over time, the instrument should reveal increased amounts of student-initiated uses of reading in the classroom.

References

Atwell, N. 1987. *In the middle*. Portsmouth, NH: Boynton/Cook.

Goodman, Y. M., D. W. Watson, & C. L. Burke. 1987. *Reading miscue inventory: Alternative procedures*. Katonah, NY: Richard C. Owen.

McKenna, M. C., & D. J. Kear. 1990. Measuring attitude toward reading: A new tool for teachers. *Reading Teacher*, 43 (9), 626-639.

Vacca, R. & J. Vacca. 1989. *Content area reading* (3rd ed.). Glenview, IL: Scott Foresman.

Name _____   Date _____

Reading Survey

1. If you had to guess...
    How many books would you say you owned? _____
    How many books would you say are in your house? _____
    How many books would you say you've read in the last month? _____

2. How did you learn to read?

    _____

    _____

    _____

3. Why do people read?

    _____

    _____

    _____

4. What does someone have to do in order to be a good reader?

    _____

    _____

    _____

5. How does a teacher decide which students are good readers?

    _____

    _____

    _____

6. What kinds of books do you like to read?

    _____

    _____

    _____

7. How do you decide which books you'll read?

_____

_____

_____

8. Have you ever reread a book? _____ If so, can you name it/them here?

_____

_____

_____

9. Do you ever read books at home for pleasure? _____ If so, how often do you read at home (for pleasure)?

_____

_____

_____

10. Who are your favorite authors? (List as many as you'd like.)

_____

_____

_____

11. Do you like to have your teacher read to you? _____ If so, is there anything special you'd like to hear?

_____

_____

_____

12. In general, how do you feel about reading?

_____

_____

_____

Reading Survey reprinted with permission of Nancie Atwell: *In The Middle* (Boynton/Cook Publishers, Portsmouth, NH, 1987).

Reading Interview: A Reader's View of the Reading Process

The *Reading Interview* is designed to be given individually and orally and is suitable for students of all ages. (An adapted version for emergent readers may be found in the Emergent Reading and Writing section of this handbook.) It uncovers the student's perceptions of the reading process, the model the student believes teachers have about reading, and how a student's learning-to-read history might have affected his or her perceptions of reading.

The first and fifth questions uncover the reading strategies that the reader can verbalize. Although you may observe the reader using strategies other than those verbalized, these are the strategies the reader is most likely to consciously rely on when he or she encounters difficulty.

Several of the questions uncover the student's notion of what an effective reader is and does. This allows the teacher to understand what the reader may be striving for in becoming a better reader; it may be that the teacher needs to change the student's view of effective reading so that the student is striving for something that will truly make him or her a more effective reader.

Finally, some of the questions uncover what it is that the student has seen teachers do to help students and what they think teachers ought to do. A teacher's actions and a student's beliefs sometimes match and sometimes do not. In either case, it is enlightening for the teacher to consider what he or she does as a teacher in light of the student's past experiences and expectations. Again, it may be that the student needs to change his or her view of what teachers can best do to help students become more effective readers.

The Coding Directions that accompany the interview are designed to be used by teachers or program coordinators who want to aggregate the information they collect from students. The codes may also help teachers understand the wide variety of possible student responses to each question, especially when a particular group of students gives only a narrow range of responses.

Name _____ Date _____

Grade _____ Interview Setting _____

Reading Interview

1. When you are reading and come to something you don't know, what do you do?

   _____

   _____

   _____

   Do you ever do anything else?

   _____

   _____

2. Who do you know who is a good reader?

   _____

3. What makes _____ a good reader?

   _____

   _____

   _____

4. Do you think _____ ever comes to something s/he doesn't know?

   _____

   _____

5. If question 4 is yes: When _____ does come to something s/he doesn't know, what do you think s/he does?

   If question 4 is no: Suppose _____ comes to something that s/he doesn't know. What do you think s/he would do?

   _____

   _____

6. If you know someone was having trouble reading, how would you help that person?

_____

_____

_____

7. What would a/your teacher do to help that person?

_____

_____

_____

8. How did you learn to read?

_____

_____

_____

9. What would you like to do better as a reader?

_____

_____

_____

10. Do you think you are a good reader? Why?

_____

_____

_____

Reading Interview by Carolyn L. Burke in *Reading Miscue Inventory: Alternative Procedures* by Y.M. Goodman, D.W. Watson, and C.L. Burke. Published by Richard C. Owen, 1987. Reprinted with permission of the publisher.

Coding Directions for *Reading Interview*

Code no more than ten interviews at a time.

    A. On the first interview in a batch of 10 or less, score questions 1, 5, 6, 7 and 9 using the "Strategies" categories.

    B. Follow step "A" for all other interviews in the batch.

    C. Then go back to the first interview in the batch and code the interview for questions 3 and 10 (the second part) using the "Reason/Evidence" categories.

    D. Follow step "C" for all other interviews in the batch.

When a student provides several answers to one question, record the codes in the order the student provided the answers.

When a student provides several answers to one question and the answers, though different, receive the same code, code the different answers only once. For example, if a student says that he or she asks his mother for words and he uses the dictionary, the two answers receive a single code—a 3 for "consult outside resources."

When it is not entirely clear what a student may mean by an answer, previous or succeeding answers may be consulted for clarification.

For interview questions 4 and 10 (the first part), record the following:

- for "Yes": Y

- for "No": N

- for any other answer: record the child's words ("sometimes," "pretty good," etc.).

For interview question 8, record the person(s) or place(s) named and next to each, the strategy(ies) used. For example:

- father: 7

- teacher: 1, 2

- school: 6

- self: 8

Coding Directions by Carolyn Burke, Lynn K. Rhodes and Curt Dudley-Marling. Reprinted with permission of the authors.

Strategies

(Questions 1, 5, 6, 7, and 9)

Code 1: Use context to determine word

Answers that fit this category refer to using textual information beyond the difficulty itself. Examples include:

- "Read on and figure it out."

- "Look at the words around it and try to figure it out from there."

- "Read the rest of the sentence."

Answers that suggest word omission as a strategy fit in this category if the reader also mentions a return to the word after omitting it. For example:

- "Skip it and try to figure it out from the rest of the sentence."

- "Skip it and come back to it."

- "Skip it and once you've read the whole story, you can figure it out."

Code 2: Examine word parts

Answers that fit in this category refer to examining or learning various word parts: letters, the alphabet, syllables, vowels, endings, even "parts" or "pieces." In addition, answers like the following are included:

- "Sound it out."

- "Spell it out."

- "Try to pronounce it."

Code 3: Consult outside resources

Answers that fit this category refer to a source of information outside the reader, either another person (frequently a teacher, parent, or another student) or a written source such as a dictionary. (This category is not to be used to code questions 4 or 5 unless the student specifies that the person providing the help obtains the assistance of a second resource as defined above.)

Code 4: Omit

Answers that refer to the complete omission of a word while reading fit into this category. For example:

- "If it's too hard, I skip it."

- "Just pass the word up."

If a reference is also made to returning to the word after it has been omitted, the answer is classified as "Use context to determine word." The only exceptions are those answers indicating that the child has deliberately omitted a word and then returned to it only to examine word parts rather than to use meaning:

- "Skip the word and go on and then come back to it and then sound it out."

Such an answer would be classified as both "Omit" and "Examine word parts."

Code 5: Word meaning

Answers that fit this category refer to an explanation of the meaning of a word or suggest that word meaning ought to receive attention.

Code 6: Classroom procedures

Answers that fit this general category refer to 1) physical movement, 2) classroom materials or groupings, or 3) diagnostic procedures. Physical movement answers may refer to a change in location by someone or a lack of movement:

- "She tells me to bring the problem to her desk."

- "She'll walk over if you raise your hand."

- "She tells us to wait until she is done."

Other answers mention instructional materials (other than books) or instructional groupings or levels:

- "She gives us papers."

- "They just give me work at that level."

- "She'd put me in a lower level."

Finally, some answers suggest a focus on diagnosing a problem or providing feedback about whether something has been done correctly:

- "I figure out where they're having trouble."

- "The next time you missed it, she'd probably do the same thing (nod her head no) and then if you do it again, she'd do it again (nod her head no) until you got it right."

Code 7: Word identification

Answers that fit this category refer to information about the identification of a whole word or the practice of whole words. Only answers that treat words as wholes are categorized as "Word identification"; answers that refer to the identification of word parts are categorized as "Examine word parts." Some examples of answers in this category are:

- "Learn big words."

- "Every time I got stuck, I asked what the word would be."

- "Started off with easy words and kept getting harder."

Occasionally, answers will make a reference to words in such a way that whether the child was thinking of whole words or an examination of word parts is somewhat ambiguous. That is, the child spoke of words but might have meant an examination of word parts. Some answers that are like this and ought to be categorized "Word identification" include:

- "She wrote down words for me and asked me to read them."

- "Keep studying words."

Code 8: Read text

Answers that fit this category refer to the reading, buying, and/or borrowing of books, stories, or other text. Examples are:

- "I tried to read little books."

- "She read stories to me."

- "They bought me a whole bunch of easy and then harder books to read."

Answers that do not refer directly to books/stories/text but to situations in which it is unlikely that anything but books/stories/text would be read also fit this category. Some examples are:

- "I read out loud to my class."

- "Sometimes I just read by myself."

Code 9: Attend to reading speed

Answers that fit this category refer to increasing or decreasing the rate of reading.

Code 10: Take interest in reading

Answers that fit this category refer to concentrating on what is being read or taking an interest in what is being read.

Code 11: Unclassifiable

Unintelligible answers and answers that do not make sense are included in this category. In addition, ambiguous answers that should have been clarified by the interviewer with a follow-up question are categorized as unclassifiable. For example, if a child answered, "I just kept trying," a question like "What did you keep trying to do?" would probably have provided clarification.

Evidence/Reasons

(Questions 3 and 10)

Code 12: Reading behavior

Answers refer to a specific aspect of reading behavior as *evidence* or *reasons* that a person is a good/poor reader. The reading behavior cited may include aspects of undefined reading skills, word recognition, comprehension, the amount of reading done by the person, reading speed, oral reading intonation or pausing, use of context, or independence in reading tasks.

Code 13: Teacher recognition

Answers refer to reading group placement or material, grades, verbal comment by the teacher or some other piece of *evidence* dominated by teacher decisions or behavior.

Code 14: General inner resources

Answers refer to *reasons* beyond the reader's control: the reader's age, memory, talent for reading, intelligence, interest in reading, or certain advantages such as parents who helped the reader.

Code 15: General behavior

Answers refer to general *reasons* within the reader's control but do not refer specifically to reading and could just as well apply to tasks other than reading: effort, amount of practice or study, concentration, mood, or attention to task. However, when responses such as "I need more practice" are given that do not specify reading practice but clearly show that the response refers to reading, it should be classified as "reading behavior" (category 1) rather than "general behavior" (category 4).

Code 16: Unclassifiable

Unintelligible answers and answers that do not make sense are included in this category. In addition, circular answers that do not provide reasons or evidence but instead restate the question fit this category. (An example of a circular answer to a question: "Why are you sick?" "Because I don't feel well.") Examples of circular answers regarding reading include: "She just reads pretty good." "I can't read well."

Content Reading Interview

1. How much do you read in _____?
   content area

   What do you read? Why?

2. When you are reading in _____ and come to
   content area
   something you don't know, what do you do?

   Do you ever do anything else?

3. Who is the best reader you know in _____?
   content area

   What makes him or her a good reader in _____?
   content area

4. How good are you at reading your _____
   content area
   book(s)?

   How do you know?

5. What is the hardest part about answering the questions in the book(s)
   used in _____?
   content area

6. If you needed to study a chapter in _____ so
   content area
   you could remember the information, how would you do it?

7. Have you ever tried _____? Tell about it.
   name a study strategy

8. What do you have to do to get a good grade in _____
   content area
   class?

Content Reading Interview (Vacca & Vacca) from "An Interview for Assessing Students' Perceptions of Classroom Reading Tasks" by Karen K. Wixson, Anita B. Bosky, M. Nina Yochum, and Donna E. Alverman, *The Reading Teacher*, January 1984. Adaptation reprinted with permission of the International Reading Association.

Denver Reading Attitude Survey

Description

The *Denver Reading Attitude Survey* provides an indication of students' engagement in reading activities, their perception of the importance and utility of reading, and their confidence in themselves as readers. The survey includes a few items from the National Assessment of Educational Progress.

Instructions for Administering

So that the results of the survey are not affected by variations in reading ability, read each item aloud. Students respond to each item by circling the letter of their response.

Spanish and English versions are available. Students should complete the survey in the language they are most confident using.

Explain that the purpose of the survey is to learn students' honest feelings about reading in and out of school. Emphasize that this is not a test; there are no right or wrong answers, and the results will have no effect on grades.

As you read the items, clarify them and answer questions as needed. Also draw attention to each change in the response format.

Name _____   Grade _____

Teacher _____   Date _____

Denver Reading Attitude Survey

Make a circle around the answer that is most true for you.

How often do you do each of the following things?

	Almost every day	Once or twice a week	Once or twice a month	A few times a year	Never or hardly ever
1. Get so interested in something you're reading that you don't want to stop.	A	B	C	D	E
2. Read the newspaper.	A	B	C	D	E
3. Tell a friend about a good book.	A	B	C	D	E
4. Read on your own outside of school.	A	B	C	D	E
5. Read about something because you are curious about it.	A	B	C	D	E
6. Read more than one book by an author you like.	A	B	C	D	E

7. What kind of reader do you think you are?

    A.   A very good reader.

    B.   A good reader.

    C.   An average reader.

    D.   A poor reader.

    E.   A very poor reader.

(continued)

The following statements are true for some people. They may or may not be true for you, or they may be true for you only part of the time. How often is each of the following sentences true for you?

	Almost always	More than half the time	About half the time	Less than half the time	Never or hardly ever
8. Reading helps me learn about myself.	A	B	C	D	E
9. I feel good about how fast I can read.	A	B	C	D	E
10. Reading helps me understand why people feel or act the way they do.	A	B	C	D	E
11. I believe that reading will help me get ahead when I am no longer in school.	A	B	C	D	E
12. I feel proud about what I can read.	A	B	C	D	E
13. Reading helps me see what it might be like to live in a different place or in a different way.	A	B	C	D	E
14. Being able to read well is important to me.	A	B	C	D	E
15. I can understand what I read in school.	A	B	C	D	E
16. Other people think I read well.	A	B	C	D	E
17. I learn worthwhile things from reading books.	A	B	C	D	E

Denver Reading Attitude Survey by W. Alan Davis and Lynn K. Rhodes, 1991. Reprinted with permission of the authors.

Nombre _____ Grado _____

Maestro/a _____ Fecha _____

Encuesta Sobre Lectura de Denver

Encierre en un círculo la letra de la respuesta que sea mas cierta para usted.

¿Con qué frecuencia hace cada una de las siguientes cosas?

	Casi cada día	Una o dos veces por semana	Una o dos veces por mes	Varias veces por año	Nunca o casi nunca
1. Se interesa tanto en la lectura que no puede dejar de leer.	A	B	C	D	E
2. Lee el periódico.	A	B	C	D	E
3. Le plactica a un(a) amigo(a) de un buen libro.	A	B	C	D	E
4. Lee libros de texto (como por ejemplo de ciencias sociales o naturales).	A	B	C	D	E
5. Lee algo por curiosidad.	A	B	C	D	E
6. Lee más de un libro de algún escritor que le guste.	A	B	C	D	E

7. ¿Qué tipo de lector se considera usted?

    A.   Excelente lector.

    B.   Buen lector.

    C.   Lector regular.

    D.   Lector con problemas.

    E.   Lector con muchos problemas.

(continuado)

Las siguientes declaraciones se refieren a ciertas personas. Estas declaraciones no necesariamente son aplicables a usted, o serán ciertas solo en algunas ocasiones. ¿Con qué frecuencia es cada una de las siguientes declaraciones cierta para usted?

	Casi siempre	Más de la mitad del tiempo	Como la mitad del tiempo	Menos de la mitad del tiempo	Nunca o casi nunca
8. La lectura me ayuda a aprender de mi mismo(a).	A	B	C	D	E
9. Me gusta la rapidez con la que leo.	A	B	C	D	E
10. La lectura me ayuda a entender por qué la gente se siente o actúa de la manera en que lo hace.	A	B	C	D	E
11. Pienso que la lectura me ayudará a salir adelante cuando ya no esté en la escuela.	A	B	C	D	E
12. Me siento orgulloso(a) de lo que puedo leer.	A	B	C	D	E
13. La lectura me ayuda a ver cómo sería vivir de otra manera o en otro lugar.	A	B	C	D	E
14. El poder leer bien es importante para mi.	A	B	C	D	E
15. Entiendo mi lectura escolar.	A	B	C	D	E
16. Otra gente piensa que yo leo bien.	A	B	C	D	E
17. Aprendo cosas que valen la pena a través de libros.	A	B	C	D	E

Denver Reading Attitude Survey by W. Alan Davis and Lynn K. Rhodes, 1991. Reprinted with permission of the authors.

Elementary Reading Attitude Survey

The *Elementary Reading Attitude Survey* provides a quick indication of student attitudes toward reading. It consists of 20 items and can be administered to an entire classroom in about 10 minutes. Each item presents a brief, simply worded statement about reading, followed by four pictures of Garfield. Each pose is designed to depict a different emotional state ranging from very positive to very negative.

Administration

Begin by telling students that you wish to find out how they feel about reading. Emphasize that this is *not* a test and that there are no "right" answers. Encourage sincerity.

Distribute the survey forms and, if you wish to monitor the attitudes of specific students, ask them to write their names in the space at the top. Hold up a copy of the survey so that the students can see the first page. Point to the picture of Garfield at the far left of the first item. Ask the students to look at this same picture on their own survey form. Discuss with them the mood Garfield seems to be in (very happy). Then move to the next picture and again discuss Garfield's mood (this time, a *little* happy). In the same way, move to the third and fourth pictures and talk about Garfield's moods—a little upset and very upset. It is helpful to point out the position of Garfield's *mouth*, especially in the two middle figures.

Explain that together you will read some statements about reading and that the students should think about how they feel about each statement. They should then circle the picture of Garfield that is closest to their own feelings. (Emphasize that the students should respond according to their own feelings, not as Garfield might respond!) Read each item aloud slowly and distinctly; then read it a second time while students are thinking. Be sure to read the item *number* and to remind students of page numbers when new pages are reached.

Scoring

To score the survey, count four points for each leftmost (happiest) Garfield circled, three for each slightly smiling Garfield, two for each mildly upset Garfield, and one point for each very upset (rightmost) Garfield. Three scores for each student can be obtained: the total for the first 10 items, the total for the second 10, and a composite total. The first half of the survey relates to attitude toward recreational reading; the second half relates to attitude toward academic aspects of reading.

■ Interpretation

You can interpret scores in two ways. One is to note informally where the score falls in regard to the four nodes of the scale. A total score of 50, for example, would fall about midway on the scale, between the slightly happy and slightly upset figures, therefore indicating a relatively indifferent overall attitude toward reading. The other approach is more formal. It involves converting the raw scores into percentile ranks by means of Table 1 (McKenna and Kear, 1990). Be sure to use the norms for the right grade level and to note the column headings (Rec = recreational reading, Aca = academic reading, Tot = total score). If you wish to determine the average percentile rank for your class, average the raw scores first; then use the table to locate the percentile rank corresponding to the raw score mean. Percentile ranks cannot be averaged directly.

Elementary Reading Attitude Survey from "Measuring attitudes toward reading: A new tool for teachers" by Michael C. McKenna and D. J. Kear, *The Reading Teacher*, May 1990. Reprinted with permission of Michael C. McKenna and the International Reading Association.

Name _____ Grade _____ Date _____

Elementary Reading Attitude Survey

1. How do you feel when you read a book on a rainy Saturday?

2. How do you feel when you read a book in school during free time?

3. How do you feel about reading for fun at home?

4. How do you feel about getting a book for a present?

5. How do you feel about spending free time reading?

6. How do you feel about starting a new book?

7. How do you feel about reading during summer vacation?

8. How do you feel about reading instead of playing?

GARFIELD reprinted by permission of UFS, Inc.

9. How do you feel about going to a bookstore?

10. How do you feel about reading different kinds of books?

11. How do you feel when the teacher asks you questions about what you read?

12. How do you feel about doing reading workbook pages and worksheets?

13. How do you feel about reading in school?

14. How do you feel about reading your school books?

15. How do you feel about learning from a book?

16. How do you feel when it's time for reading class?

Reading

17. How do you feel about the stories you read in reading class?

18. How do you feel when you read out loud in class?

19. How do you feel about using a dictionary?

20. How do you feel about taking a reading test?

GARFIELD reprinted by permission of UFS, Inc.

Elementary Reading Attitude Survey
Scoring sheet

Scoring guide	
4 points	Happiest Garfield
3 points	Slightly smiling Garfield
2 points	Mildly upset Garfield
1 point	Very upset Garfield

Recreational reading   Academic reading

1. _____   11. _____

2. _____   12. _____

3. _____   13. _____

4. _____   14. _____

5. _____   15. _____

6. _____   16. _____

7. _____   17. _____

8. _____   18. _____

9. _____   19. _____

10. _____   20. _____

Raw score: _____   Raw score: _____

Full scale raw score (Recreational + Academic): _____

Percentile ranks   Recreational   _____

                        Academic   _____

                        Full scale   _____

An Inventory of Classroom Reading Use

An Inventory of Classroom Reading Use is an instrument designed to help teachers examine students' progress toward making reading an important part of their lives by exploring whether students *use* reading in their lives.

Directions:

1. Fill out the information blanks for each student with whom you want to use this questionnaire.

2. For each question, indicate with a mark on the appropriate line the degree to which the student exhibits the described reading.

3. For each question, indicate with a check mark in the appropriate box whether the described reading is initiated by you or another teacher, by the student, or by both.

4. Fill out the questionnaire at intervals that you find helpful in planning instruction. It may be helpful to fill out this questionnaire approximately a month after the school year begins and about midway through the year in order to plan instruction. Or you may find it helpful to use the questionnaire toward the end of each grading period.

5. The questionnaire may also be useful for program evaluation purposes when a chief goal of instruction is to develop lifelong readers. Consider using the questionnaire at intervals that allow you to show your progress with students toward that goal. The information is helpful in discussing your program with administrators and in conferring with parents and others concerned about the student's progress.

Questions to consider:

1. Are students having enough reading opportunities?

2. Are students reading a wide range of materials?

3. Are students developing the skills necessary to choose and find their own reading materials?

4. Are students finding reading an enjoyable part of their lives?

5. Do students consider reading meaningful and relevant to their lives?

6. Is the curriculum you have established conducive to the above goals? (Check "teacher-initiated" column.)

7. Are students moving toward independence in relation to the above goals? (Is there a change in scores over time?)

8. Are students moving toward independence in relation to the above goals? (Check "student-initiated" column.)

9. Are the scores lower for low ability students? If so, is the curriculum you have established for the low ability students conducive to growth in relation to the above goals?

10. Compare the data from several students whose scores are quite different and think about why they are different. What can you do to affect the situation?

Name _____ Grade _____

Teacher _____ Date _____

An Inventory of Classroom Reading Use

To what extent does the student:

		Not at all	A little	To some extent	To a large extent	To a great extent	Teacher-initiated	Student-initiated
1.	Utilize available environmental print? (posters, cafeteria menu, notices to go home)	A	B	C	D	E	☐	☐
2.	Seek specific information from printed material? (maps, yellow pages, directions)	A	B	C	D	E	☐	☐
3.	Gather related information for a specific purpose from a variety of sources?	A	B	C	D	E	☐	☐
4.	Engage in a wide variety of book reading?	A	B	C	D	E	☐	☐
5.	Engage in reading materials at various difficulty levels? (easy to hard for child)	A	B	C	D	E	☐	☐
6.	Seek/follow up the reading of a piece of material with related reading? (another book by the same author, another book on the same topic)	A	B	C	D	E	☐	☐
7.	Choose to read during "choice" time?	A	B	C	D	E	☐	☐
8.	Engage fully in reading during sustained silent reading periods?	A	B	C	D	E	☐	☐

Comments:

_____

Developed by CAWLs (Coordinators/Consultants Applying Whole Language)

Comprehension Checklists

Checklist Items
Form A: Comprehension Assessment
Form B: Comprehension Assessment
Form C: Comprehension Assessment

Instead of providing already developed comprehension checklists, checklist items and three different formats for presenting selected checklist items have been provided. Consider your own situation and decide which checklist items and formats will be of most use to you. The next four pages include:

1. Checklist items. The list of checklist items is infinitely malleable; you can add to it, take away from it, and reword any item on it to best reflect your instructional goals and circumstances. Instead of using too many items, select and revise those which are most important to assess at this time. Reconsider the items several times during the year and consider constructing different checklists for different students or groups of students.

2. A multiple setting checklist for a single student (Form A). For each student whose comprehension you want to assess, you'll need a separate copy of Form A. Each vertical slot is labeled with the text and the date, permitting the same checklist to be used multiple times for the same student. Marks corresponding to descriptors (i.e., +: to a great extent, ✔: to some extent, −: not at all, blank space or 0: not observed in this setting) are placed in the blanks next to the items. The notes at the end may include important details not captured by the checklist, including the context in which comprehension was assessed.

3. A single setting checklist for a single student (Form B). You'll need a copy of Form B not only for each student but also for each comprehension assessment you do for a single student. This format is most useful for teachers who do more formal assessment on a regularly scheduled basis. Marks corresponding to descriptors may be used as in Form A. Unlike Form A, there is space in Form B for a comment about each checklist item, yielding more detailed clues concerning how to support the student's comprehension development.

4. A single setting checklist for a group of students (Form C). Form C is useful for teachers who want to collect information about students' comprehension during group literacy events such as a book discussion. The title of the book being discussed and the context in which it is discussed may be recorded at the top of the page. Marks corresponding to descriptors must again be used. Comments may be recorded at the bottom of the sheet.

Checklist Items

The phrases below may be used as items on the checklist formats that follow. The phrases are categorized as "before reading," "during reading," or "after reading" and some take place at any point in the reading process.

Before Reading

- Uses titles, pictures, captions, graphs, blurbs to predict.

- Uses background knowledge to predict.

- Intrinsically motivated to engage in reading.

During Reading

- Is aware when text doesn't make sense.

- Uses preceding text to predict.

- Reads to answer own questions about text.

- Reads "between the lines."

- Understands and uses structure of text.

- Rereads when comprehension difficult.

- Changes reading mode (silent & oral) when comprehension difficult.

- Gets help when comprehension difficult.

- Reads at an appropriate rate for the text.

- Able to identify concepts, language, or vocabulary that interfere with comprehension.

- Searches efficiently for specific information.

After Reading

- Extends comprehension through writing.

- Extends comprehension through discussion.

- Recalls important information.

- Recalls sufficient information.

- Summarizes main points.

- Adjusts what is shared about the text for the audience.
- Identifies story elements in text (characters, setting, problem, episodes, resolution).
- States appropriate theme for story.
- Uses text to support statements & conclusions.
- Compares characters in text.
- Retells fluently (length & coherence).
- Links story episodes in narrative; facts in expository text.
- Uses author's language in retelling.
- Uses own "voice" in retelling.

Before, During, or After Reading

- Compares characters or incidents to self or experiences.
- Compares this text to other texts.
- Compares this text to media other than text.
- Uses text to support statements & conclusions.
- Identifies point-of-view.
- Distinguishes between fact and opinion.

Name _____

Form A: Comprehension Assessment

Checklist Items	Text read and date					

Notes

Date:

Date:

Date:

Date:

Date:

Date:

Name _____   Date _____

Title of text _____

Context _____

Form B: Comprehension Assessment

Checklist Items	+ ✓ − 0	Comments

Title of text _____

Date _____   Context _____

Form C: Comprehension Assessment

Checklist Items	Students' Names								

Notes

Miscue Analysis

Classroom Reading Miscue Assessment
In-Process Reading Strategies

Analysis of reading miscues, or deviations from text, provides teachers with a great deal of information about students' use of three language systems (graphophonics, syntax, and semantics) in addition to information about students' reading strategies. The key resource for miscue analysis is:

> Goodman, Y. M., D. W. Watson, & C. L. Burke (1987). *Reading miscue inventory: Alternative procedures.* New York: Richard C. Owen.

The *Classroom Reading Miscue Assessment* was developed by a Denver group, Coordinators/Consultants Applying Whole Language (CAWLs), in order to help classroom teachers efficiently gather miscue data. Using the CRMA, a teacher can record data from listening to a student orally read and retell a complete passage of 300-500 words in approximately 10-15 minutes. Often, teachers collect and record data on one or two students per day using time during sustained silent reading, Reading Workshop, "specials," recess, or planning periods.

In Part I of the CRMA, the teacher tallies each sentence as semantically acceptable or unacceptable as the student reads. To tally sentences, the teacher considers whether each sentence makes sense after self-corrections are taken into account. By dividing the number of semantically acceptable sentences by the total number of sentences read, a comprehending (in-process comprehension) score may be figured, providing an indication of the degree to which the student constructs meaning effectively in the process of reading. Part I is the same procedure as the Reading Conference Form found in Goodman, Watson, and Burke (1987).

While tallying semantic acceptability, a teacher can also make general observations about the student's strategy and cue use while reading. When the student finishes reading the text, these observations are recorded in Part II. For instructional planning, it is sufficient for the teacher to be internally consistent in determining behaviors for the ratings. If the instrument is to be used across classrooms or teachers or aggregated for policy-making purposes, rating sessions need to be held. In rating sessions, teachers listen to tapes of a variety of readers, then rate and discuss them in order to achieve consistent reliability among raters. Guidelines for each rating could be written using a process similar to that used to define descriptors for scoring writing samples analytically.

After a student has completed the oral reading, the teacher first listens to the student's unaided retelling and then uses question probes as necessary. Probes should not give further information about the passage and are best framed using the categories suggested by Part III. For example, "You've told about event X and event Z. What happened in between those two events?" The teacher's judgments about the retelling are recorded in Part III using the appropriate narrative or expository descriptors. Again, the teacher needs to strive for internal consistency or interrater reliability in his or her judgments.

The *In-Process Reading Strategies* checklist may be used to keep records on an individual student's use of various strategies observed during the reading process. Most often, it is used during a conference in which the student reads text aloud. However, it may also be used in a conference in which the student is asked to reflect on silent reading he or she is doing. Keeping records of the texts read allows the teacher to see if strategies change from one text to another. Keeping records of the date on which the checklist is used allows the teacher to observe the extent to which the student is making progress in using a variety of strategies.

"Miscue Analysis in the Classroom" by Lynn K. Rhodes and Nancy L. Shanklin, *The Reading Teacher*, November 1990. Reprinted with permission of the authors and the International Reading Association.

Classroom Reading Miscue Assessment

The checklist is designed to help teachers identify what reading strategies a student uses and with what degree of frequency. The instrument will guide teachers to plan instruction that will improve students' proficiency with effective reading strategies. In this assessment procedure, a child reads a whole story to a teacher while the teacher records how effectively the child strives to make sense of the story. Say to the child, "I need to learn what you know about reading and what more you are ready to learn about reading. To do that, I'd like you to read this story/article/information out loud while I make some notes. As you read, do what you normally do when you are reading by yourself. Pretend I am not here. When you finish I'll ask you to tell me what you read."

Directions:

Fill in child's name, the date the child reads, the child's present grade level assignment, and your name.

There are two options in selecting material for the child to read.

1. A complete story from the basal in which he or she normally reads. List the publisher of the basal, the level of the basal, and the title of the story the child reads.

   Or

2. A children's literature (a story) or content (an expository text) selection. To select the appropriate level of difficulty, use this guideline: the child should not make more than *one* meaning-changing error in ten words, i.e., the child should not read a word that changes the meaning of the text and leave it uncorrected more than once in every ten words. List the title of the story the child reads.

Part I

The goal of proficient readers is to make sense. The analysis of Part I will indicate to what degree the child has the goal of making sense.

As the child reads, tally if each sentence makes sense or does not make sense as the child last read it.

- This does not mean that a child has to read every word in a sentence correctly. If the child maintains the meaning of the sentence, even though some words are not read exactly, the sentence should be counted as semantically acceptable. For example, if the text states, "He had a hard time getting into *his* house at night," and the reader reads, "He had a hard time getting into *the* house at night," the sentence is semantically acceptable. If the text states, "He was *hungry* enough to eat anything," and the reader reads (without self-correcting), "He was *hurry* enough to eat anything," this sentence is not semantically acceptable.

- When marking whether a sentence is semantically acceptable, consider the sentence as the child finally reads it. Children may read words initially that don't make sense but correct them before going on to the next sentence. Give them credit for these rereadings and corrections if the sentence subsequently makes sense. For example, the sentence "Soon the table was so full that *he* began to put them on his bookshelves," was first read as "Soon the table was so full that *the* began to put them on his bookshelves." As the child discovered that the miscue didn't make sense with what followed in the sentence, he went back and read it with the correct wording. This sentence should be marked semantically acceptable.

- Often a child makes more than one miscue in a sentence. If he or she corrects one or more of the miscues but still leaves one or more miscues that disrupt meaning, the sentence is still semantically *un*acceptable. (However, do keep in mind the self-corrections the child is making so that you can include that information in Part II.)

- In marking whether a sentence is semantically acceptable, also consider proper intonation and punctuation. For example, if a child disrupts meaning by running through a period without adding an acceptable conjunction or by turning a statement into a question, the sentence is not semantically acceptable.

Count the number of tallies in each row and list the sum in the Total box. Then add the two Total boxes to determine the total number of sentences read.

To predict how well the child was comprehending the story while reading, compute the percentage of sentences that made sense as the child read.

▨ Part II

This section lists four strategies proficient readers use to make sense of a text and three behaviors that interfere with comprehension of a text. Observing the child's use of each strategy helps you plan instruction for the reader.

- With what frequency does the reader give some indication that the text doesn't make sense as s/he reads, even though s/he isn't able to do anything about it?

- With what frequency does the reader replace words in the text with other words that make sense?

  Example: "Goldilocks ran like lightning out of the three bears' *house*."
  Reader: "Goldilocks ran like lighting out of the three bears' *home*."
  "Home" is a meaningful substitution for "house."

- With what frequency does the reader go back and self-correct miscues that changed the text meaning?

- With what frequency do the child's eyes take in pictures or other visual clues? For example, the child can't use information from pictures if his or her hand is covering the pictures while reading.

- With what frequency does the child replace words in the text with other words that do not make sense in the sentence or in the story and give no indication of being uncomfortable with the lack of meaning?

  Example: "He liked to cook and *could* make good things to eat."
  Reader: "He liked to cook and *cold* make good things to eat."

- With what frequency does the child leave out words that carry meaning for the sentence or story and give no indication that meaning is lost?

- With what frequency does the child use graphophonic information to the exclusion of information about what would make sense, might be expected, or would sound right in English?

▊ Part III

One of the best measures in comprehension of the reader's ability to make sense of text is a child's unaided retelling of what has been read. When the child finishes reading, say to the child, *"Tell me everything you remember about what you read."* After the child has told you what he or she can, use the probe, *"Is there anything more you remember about the story?"* Only *after* the child has totally finished the unaided retelling should you consider asking questions to further probe what the child remembers. (Questioning should be considered optional.) A complete retelling of narrative text should include information about character, setting, events, plot, and theme and indicate the child's grasp of the text structure. A complete retelling of expository text should include major concepts, generalizations, specific information, and logical structuring. A partial retelling may reflect the broad sense of the text but lack structure or detail. A child who makes no attempt to reconstruct what he or she has read likely indicates an inability to retell the text or a lack of comprehension.

Reader's name _____ Date _____

Grade level _____ Teacher _____

Selection read _____

Classroom Reading Miscue Assessment

I. What percent of the sentences read make sense?

	Sentence by sentence tally	Total
Number of semantically acceptable sentences	_____	_____
Number of semantically unacceptable sentences	_____	_____

% Comprehending score:

$$\frac{\text{Number of semantically acceptable sentences}}{\text{Total number of sentences read}} \quad \text{x } 100 \quad = \quad \underline{\hspace{1cm}} \%$$

II. In what ways is the reader constructing meaning?

	Seldom	Sometimes	Often	Usually	Always
A. Recognizes when miscues have disrupted meaning	1	2	3	4	5
B. Logically substitutes	1	2	3	4	5
C. Self-corrects errors that disrupt meaning	1	2	3	4	5
D. Uses picture and/or other visual clues	1	2	3	4	5

In what ways is the reader disrupting meaning?

	Seldom	Sometimes	Often	Usually	Always
A. Substitutes words that don't make sense	1	2	3	4	5
B. Makes omissions that disrupt meaning	1	2	3	4	5
C. Relies too heavily on graphophonic cues	1	2	3	4	5

III. If narrative text is used:

	No		Partial		Yes
A. Character recall	1	2	3	4	5
B. Character development	1	2	3	4	5
C. Setting	1	2	3	4	5
D. Relationship of events	1	2	3	4	5
E. Plot	1	2	3	4	5
F. Theme	1	2	3	4	5
G. Overall retelling	1	2	3	4	5

If expository text is used:

	No		Partial		Yes
A. Major concepts	1	2	3	4	5
B. Generalizations	1	2	3	4	5
C. Specific information	1	2	3	4	5
D. Logical structuring	1	2	3	4	5
E. Overall retelling	1	2	3	4	5

Developed by Denver Coordinators/Consultants Applying Whole Language.

Name _____

In-Process Reading Strategies

E = Uses strategy in a consistently *E*ffective way.

S = Strategy is *S*ometimes used effectively and sometimes ineffectively.

I = Uses strategy in consistently *I*neffective way.

N = *N*ot observed to use strategy.

	Text & Date	Text & Date	Text & Date	Text & Date	Text & Date	Text & Date
Looks back						
Rereads						
Skips						
Substitutes word						
Asks for help						
Uses graphophonic cues						
Uses pictures/visual cues						
Uses context						
Uses background information						
Self-corrects miscues						
Recognizes miscue						

Notes

Developed by Lynn K. Rhodes, University of Colorado at Denver.

Self-Assessments of Reading

Drop Everything and Read
Book Choice
Literature Discussion
Visualizing
Word Strategies
Comprehension Strategies
What I Do Well in Reading/What I'm Working on in Reading

The self-assessments that follow are only a few of those that teachers have used successfully to engage students in considering what they are learning and what they are responsible for as readers. Like every other form of assessment teachers use, these were designed to directly reflect and gauge the impact of instruction on students' reading.

Self-assessments have two purposes. First, they provide a way for the teacher to encourage the student to become responsible for what has been taught and what is expected of him or her as a result. Second, the students' responses provide rich data for the teacher in determining the next steps in instructional planning. They reveal students' understanding of what the teacher has taught and often provide hints about what else needs to be taught.

Some of the self-assessments are analogous versions of the teacher observation forms presented in the next section. Involving both teacher and student in assessing the same aspect of reading results in data from two points of view. Often the student's and teacher's data corroborate one another, but when they do not, the teacher can see that the student may not be learning or may be learning something different from what the teacher intended or assumed.

You will notice that the self-assessments tend to be quite short. We suggest keeping them to half a page with no more than three questions (fewer if possible). Even when there is more than a single question, the questions usually focus on the same aspect of reading, asking the student to look at it from different angles.

Other examples of self-assessment may be found in *Windows Into Literacy*.

Name _____ Date _____

Drop Everything and Read (DEAR)

1. How much time did you spend reading during DEAR time today?

   all the time   most of the time   some of the time   not at all

2. If you didn't spend all the time reading, why didn't you?

   _____

   _____

3. What will help you so that you'll spend all your time reading next time
   we have DEAR time?

   _____

   _____

Cut here--

Name _____ Date _____

Book Choice

1. What book did you choose to read?

   _____

2. Is the book challenging you to be a better reader?

   _____

3. Why?

   _____

   _____

   _____

   _____

Name _____ Date _____

Title of book discussed _____

Literature Discussion

1. How much did you participate in the discussion today?

   about the right amount   too much   not at all   too little

2. What was an important contribution you made to the discussion?

   _____

   _____

3. What was an important idea expressed by someone else in the group during the discussion? (Identify the person and tell what he or she said.)

   _____

   _____

   _____

Cut here -

Name _____ Date _____

Title of reading material _____

Visualizing

1. For the last week, we have been working on making pictures in our heads. How often were you able to do that when you read by yourself today?

   _____

2. Give an example of a picture you made in your head while you were reading today.

   _____

   _____

   _____

   _____

Name _____ Date _____

What you read today _____

Word Strategies

1. What strategies from the list below did you use today to read words that were difficult for you? (Underline the strategies you used and circle the strategies you used a lot.)

    - Thought about what made sense in the sentence.
    - Reread the sentences before the difficult word.
    - Read beyond the difficult word.
    - Used information from pictures or graphs.

2. Give one example of how you figured out a difficult word. (Write the sentence the word was in and underline the word. Then tell how you figured out the word. Be specific so I can see just how you were thinking!)

    _____

    _____

    _____

Cut here---

Name _____ Date _____

What you read today _____

Word Strategies

1. List the strategies you used to figure out words when you were reading today.

    _____

    _____

2. Write down a sentence that had a word you had trouble with and underline the word.

    _____

    _____

3. Tell what you did to figure out what this word meant.

    _____

    _____

Name _____ Date _____

Book Title _____

Comprehension Strategies

1. Underline all the strategies you used today to help yourself understand the book you are reading. Circle the strategy you used the most.
   - I thought about what I already knew.
   - I made predictions and read to find out if they came true.
   - I reread what I didn't understand.
   - I made pictures in my head.
   - I asked someone to explain what I didn't understand.

2. Give an example of how you used one of the strategies you underlined or circled.

   _____

   _____

   _____

Cut here- -

Name _____ Date _____

Book Title _____

Comprehension Strategies

1. What strategies did you use today to help yourself understand the book you are reading?

   _____

   _____

2. Explain how one of the strategies you listed helped you understand something in the book.

   _____

   _____

   _____

What I Do Well in Reading

Date	

What I'm Working on in Reading

Date	

Ongoing Observations of Reading

Drop Everything and Read
Book Choice
Literature Discussion
Reading Strategies

The forms that follow are designed to help you observe and record information about students as they are involved in particular ongoing classroom activities. You don't need to ask the students to do anything different from what they usually do in order to make the observations.

The forms are analogous to those provided as examples in the "Self-Assessments in Reading" section that precedes this. As we said there, they may be used to corroborate what students perceive and/or observe about themselves. The forms are examples only; you will be able to think of many others that may inform your instruction more effectively.

These forms are valuable not only in planning instruction but also in focusing your observations. Just deciding what you want to observe in order to construct a form such as the examples here will aid you in focusing your observation.

Like the self-assessments, the observation forms only require the collection of a small portion of the data that might be recorded. Most teachers find that their observations are sharper if they don't try to observe too many aspects of reading at once. If you use such observation forms and change them frequently, you can still collect the wide range of data you are interested in over time.

Name _____ Date _____

Reading Material _____ No. minutes _____

Drop Everything and Read (DEAR)

1. How much time did the student spend reading during DEAR time today?

   all the time   most of the time   some of the time   not at all

2. If not all the time, what appeared to be the source of difficulty?

   _____

   _____

3. Source of difficulty determined through: observation   interview

Cut here -

Name _____ Date _____

Book Title _____ No. minutes _____

Book Choice

Challenge level* and comment _____

_____

_____

_____

_____

_____

_____

*Challenge level = Too difficult (D), Just right or challenging (C), or Too easy (E).

Group _____ Date _____

Literature Discussion

1. What group discussion strategies* are being used well? (When possible, note student using strategy.)

   _____

   _____

   _____

2. What discussion strategies does the group need to have brought to its attention?

   _____

   _____

   _____

* Discussion strategies: level of participation, staying on topic, contributing appropriate information, encouraging others to contribute, listening actively, looking at the speaker, considering other opinions, asking for clarification, summarizing, speaking clearly and loudly, referring to others' ideas, using members' names, etc.

Cut here- -

Name _____ Date _____

Reading Strategies

1. What reading strategies did the student use today?

   _____

   _____

   _____

2. What reading strategies need to be given more attention?

   _____

   _____

   _____

2

Writing

Interviews and Attitude Surveys

Writing Survey
Writing Interview
Denver Writing Attitude Survey
An Inventory of Classroom Writing Use

Like reading interviews and attitude surveys, writing interviews and attitude surveys are most often in either an open-ended format or a Lickert scale format. Examples of each kind are included here.

The *Writing Survey* is an adaption of the reading and writing surveys Nancie Atwell used with her middle school students (Atwell, 1987). Students' written responses to the questions enable a teacher to understand their perceptions of writing and writing instruction (like the *Writing Interview* that follows), but it focuses on the students' writing habits, interests, and attitudes toward writing. The open-ended format of the survey provides rich information when students fully respond to it. If a student does not fully respond, it is helpful to follow up with an oral interview. When using this survey, consider revisions that will elicit information of importance to you.

The *Writing Interview* is intended as an oral interview. It was developed by Catherine M. Felknor, an independent consultant from Boulder, Colorado, for use by Adams District 12, a suburb of Denver. Felknor used Burke's *Reading Interview* as a basis for its development. In addition to tapping students' attitudes about themselves as writers, the interview also provides information about students' perceptions of writing and writing instruction.

The coding system that accompanies the interview was designed to be used by teachers or program supervisors who want to aggregate the information they collect from students. It may also be used to help teachers understand the wide variety of possible responses, particularly when their students provide only a narrow range of responses.

The *Denver Writing Attitude Survey* has a Lickert scale format. It was developed by W. Alan Davis and Lynn K. Rhodes and administered as part of a research project conducted by ten University of Colorado at Denver researchers in forty fourth- and fifth-grade classrooms and has been revised on the basis of the research data. The survey is provided in both English and Spanish.

An Inventory of Classroom Writing Use was adapted by Lori L. Conrad, a teacher in Douglas County, Colorado, from *An Inventory of Classroom Reading Use*. It may be used to examine students' progress toward making writing an important part of their classroom lives by exploring how and how much students use writing in the classroom.

Besides indicating the degree to which the student uses writing in the particular way suggested by each item, the instrument also provides a means of indicating whether this use is initiated by the teacher, by the student, or both. This allows the teacher to assess his or her own initiation of the use of writing for a variety of purposes in the classroom and to assess whether the student has independently initiated use of writing for particular purposes. Over time, the instrument should reveal increased amounts of student-initiated uses of writing in the classroom.

Reference

Atwell, N. 1987. *In the middle*. Portsmouth, NH: Heinemann.

Name _____   Date _____

Teacher _____   Grade _____

Writing Survey

1. Are you a writer? _____

   (If your answer is YES, answer question 2a. If your answer is NO, answer 2b.)

2a. How did you learn to write?

   _____

   _____

2b. How do people learn to write?

   _____

   _____

3. Why do people write?

   _____

   _____

4. What do you think a good writer needs to do in order to write well?

   _____

   _____

   _____

5. How does your teacher decide which pieces of writing are the good ones?

   _____

   _____

   _____

6. What kinds of writing do you like to do?

   _____

   _____

   _____

7. How do you decide what to write?

_____

_____

_____

8. Do you ever revise or edit a piece of writing? If so, describe what you do.

_____

_____

_____

_____

9. Do you ever write at home just because you want to? _____
   If so, how often do you write at home (just because you want to)?

_____

_____

_____

_____

10. Who or what has influenced your writing? How?

_____

_____

_____

_____

11. Do you like to have others read your writing? _____ Who?

_____

_____

12. In general, how do you feel about writing?

_____

_____

_____

Writing Survey reprinted and adapted with permission of Nancie Atwell: *In the Middle* (Boynton/Cook Publishers, Portsmouth, NH, 1987).

Writing Interview: A Writer's View of the Writing Process

The *Writing Interview*, developed by Catherine M. Felknor, is designed to be given individually and orally. It consists of nine questions intended to uncover the student's perceptions of writing and the writing process and how the student's learning-to-write history might have affected his or her perceptions of writing.

Following the interview itself is a page of "Additional Pointers for Conducting the *Writing Interview*." These are ideas for follow-up questions that will help clarify students' responses if they are vague or ambiguous.

Next to each question on the *Writing Interview* is a set of three codes:

- MT: Mechanical/Technical
- PDT: Product
- PCS: Process

Each of the codes is followed by a number that corresponds to the question number on the interview. (Thus, 2.2 stands for the second part of the second question.)

The three codes for mechanical/technical, product, and process are defined on the "*Writing Interview* Coding Guide." The coding guide also provides information about how the codes are to be entered in the blanks on the *Writing Interview*. In essence, the codes help a teacher analyze each response to determine if the student is revealing a focus on the mechanical or technical aspects of writing, on aspects of writing having to do with the written product, or on aspects of writing having to do with the process of writing. These codes may be used by teachers or program coordinators who want to aggregate the information they collect from students or who want to determine the primary focus of each interviewed student. The codes may also help teachers understand the wide variety of possible responses to each question, especially when a group of students gives only a narrow range of responses.

Finally, the chart that categorizes typical student responses by focus will prove helpful in thinking about and clarifying instructional needs in writing. It has been used in staff development efforts linked to the *Writing Interview*.

Name _____ Date _____

Grade _____ Interview setting _____

Writing Interview

1. What is writing?

MT 1.1 _____ _____

PDT 1.1 _____

PCS 1.1 _____ _____

2. Among the students you know, who do you think is a good
   writer? (How easy for S to identify—circle one: difficult,
   mixed, easy.) What makes him or her a good writer?

MT 2.1 _____ _____

PDT 2.1 _____

PCS 2.1 _____ _____

What problems does he or she have when writing?

MT 2.2 _____ _____

PDT 2.2 _____

PCS 2.2 _____ _____

What do you think he or she does to solve the problem?

MT 2.3 _____ _____

PDT 2.3 _____

PCS 2.3 _____ _____

3. Among the published authors you know about (books
   you have read or that teacher/parent has read to you),
   who do you think is a good writer?

MT 3.1 _____ _____

PDT 3.1 _____

PCS 3.1 _____ _____

What makes him or her a good writer? (Why do you like
his or her writing/books?)

MT 3.2 _____ _____

PDT 3.2 _____

PCS 3.2 _____ _____

4. Think about when you first learned to write stories.
   Who helped you learn to write them?

MT 4.1 _____ _____

PDT 4.1 _____

PCS 4.1 _____ _____

How did they (he or she) help you?

MT 4.2 _____

PDT 4.2 _____

PCS 4.2 _____

5. When you are writing and you have a problem (or get stuck) what do you do?

MT 5.1 _____

PDT 5.1 _____

PCS 5.1 _____

6. What do you really like about your writing?

MT 6.1 _____

PDT 6.1 _____

PCS 6.1 _____

What would you like to improve about your writing?

MT 6.2 _____

PDT 6.2 _____

PCS 6.2 _____

7. Tell me about some writing you did last year. What did you really like about it?

MT 7.1 _____

PDT 7.1 _____

PCS 7.1 _____

How has your writing changed from last year to this year?

MT 7.2 _____

PDT 7.2 _____

PCS 7.2 _____

8. Are you a good writer? (no, mixed/not sure, yes) Why?

MT 8.1 _____

PDT 8.1 _____

PCS 8.1 _____

9. Do you like writing? (no, mixed/not sure, yes) Why?

MT 9.1 _____

PDT 9.1 _____

PCS 9.1 _____

The Writing Interview: A Writer's View of the Writing Process by Catherine M. Felknor. Reprinted with permission of the author.

Writing

Additional Pointers for Conducting the *Writing Interview*

1. If the student mentions asking for help, see if the student can clarify the type of help or the purpose of the help.

2. If the student mentions sounding out words, find out what the student means by sounding out words. If the clarification has a phonetic emphasis, code the answer MT; if the clarification has to do with invented or temporary spelling, code the answer PCS.

3. If the student mentions taking time, find out what the student means by taking time.

4. If the student mentions practicing, clarify the nature and/or purpose of the practice.

5. If the student mentions trying hard, find out what the student means by trying hard.

6. If the student says he or she "learned a lot about writing" or "learned more," clarify what was learned.

7. If the student says he or she "writes good," or "helped my writing," find out what the student means by "good" or how his or her writing was "helped."

8. If the student makes reference to drawing pictures or illustrations, determine if the student is focusing on drawing skill, the impact on the book (e.g., making it a better book), or helping to tell or understand the story.

9. If the student mentions using the dictionary, determine if the student is using the dictionary while writing the first draft or during the editing process.

10. If the student mentions working with a friend, find out the nature of the work and/or how they are cooperating.

11. When the student uses the word "someone," find out if he or she is talking about another student, teacher, parent, sibling.

Coding Guide for *Writing Interview*

Each response is scored in terms of the degree of emphasis in three areas:

- MT: Mechanical/technical focus
- PDT: Product focus
- PCS: Process focus

For each of these areas a student can be acting at Level One or Level Two. If a student offers a response that is nonscorable, leave the space blank. If a student clearly indicates "no" or "none" or provides no indication of any focus on this area, mark zero.

Mechanical/Technical Focus

0 = None; no indication of any focus on this area.

1 = Reference to a general nonspecific skill; to general appearance; to physical items/tools used; or to location, class, or time (e.g., do cursive; writing looks good; use paper & pencil; copy off board; follow directions; ABCs; practice).

2 = Reference to a specific skill(s) or to a specific characteristic(s) of the writing (e.g., finger spaces; spacing; spelling; penmanship; punctuation; divide words; use dictionary; practice letters).

Product Focus

0 = None; no indication of any focus on this area.

1 = Reference to any topic/content; to amount or type of information; to type of writing (e.g., story, poem); to length; to completing product.

2 = Reference to quality; to language or words used; description of characters, events, or nature of writing (e.g., funny, interesting); to books published, books completed, or book fair; to parts of book (e.g., chapters, table of contents); to impact of writing.

Process Focus

0 = None; no indication of any focus on this area.

1 = Implied interaction (e.g., talk about it, ask for help); reaction to doing writing (e.g., it's fun, interesting, enjoy it); general reference to step in process (e.g., choose topic, get started).

2 = Explicit interaction (e.g., listen to others, ask others for ideas or suggestions); describe working strategies (e.g., write down several ideas, use my imagination, read work over); reaction elaborated.

Coding Chart for *Writing Interview*

MECHANICAL FOCUS

Level	Logistics	Appearance	Skill	Format
1	Time of class Location of class Use paper/pencil Seat work	I (we) do printing I (we) do cursive ABCs Writing looks good Erase & start over Size; spacing Looks neat or sloppy Speed, fast, slow	Tracing Copy off board Copy words/letters Write or copy name Dictation by teacher (what teacher says) Drawing (w/emphasis on artistic skill)	Write words Layout of paper (e.g., name at top) Write sentences
2	Do worksheet Complete assignment Follow directions	Letter formation (print or cursive) Practicing letters Writing letters accurately/poorly Any reference to practice Penmanship Easy to read (writing/printing clear)	Specific skill: · capitals · punctuation · divide words · spelling · grammar Use of dictionary Sound out words · phonetic skill	Write sentences Write paragraphs Do outline Layout of paper w/more requirements

PRODUCT FOCUS

Level	Topic/Content	Amount/Type Info	Type of Writing	Recognition of Product
1	General/vague/limited reference (e.g., snow, my dog, summer vaca- tion, football, etc.) Name/title of product Name character(s)	Length · # of words · # of products · # of pages Word selection looking for word can't think of word	Story Poem Essay Autobiography Short Story	Teacher (other) said it was good Received good grade
2	Elaboration of topic or content (e.g., descrip- tion of characters, events or more detail re: topic)	Style Vocabulary Illustration (make better product) Use more than one language Story sounds real	Nature of writing funny, sad interesting clarity/detail Some elaboration of types listed above	Reference to completed work Parts of book/work (chapters, table of con- tents, etc.) Book in library or book fair Using product as model

PROCESS FOCUS

Level	Steps in Process	Reaction to Doing Writing	Interact With Others	Reference to Self
1	General reference to step (choose topic, do draft, revise) Do drawing, then tell story Do drawing to illustrate story Edit	It's fun to do It's interesting I enjoy doing it Simple, brief, no elabora- tion	Implied interaction w/o specific reference (talk about it) Listen to stories Working w/friend	Vague or general reference w/o specifics or elabora- tion (write what I want)
2	Describe process strategy(ies) (write down several ideas, use imagi- nation, read work over, use invented spelling, keep going, plan story) List steps	Elaboration of reaction to doing writing Writing outside of school/assignment Finish one story/piece, do another	Explicit interaction w/ref- erence to specific type of interaction (ask for sug- gestions or ideas, or oth- ers' questions about their story, etc.) Communication function of writing	Reference to self w/more detail (write about how I feel, helps me to think, like/ask to read my sto- ries Reliance on self as source of information Unique/different

Denver Writing Attitude Survey

Description

The *Denver Writing Attitude Survey* provides an indication of students' engagement in writing activities, their perception of the importance and utility of writing, and their confidence in themselves as writers. The survey includes a few items from the National Assessment of Educational Progress.

Instructions for Administering

So that the results of the survey are not affected by variations in reading ability, read each item aloud. Students respond to each item by circling the letter of their response.

Spanish and English versions are available. Students should complete the survey in the language they are most confident using.

Explain that the purpose of the survey is to learn students' honest feelings about reading in and out of school. Emphasize that this is not a test; there are no right or wrong answers, and the results will have no effect on grades.

As you read the items, clarify them and answer questions as needed. Also draw attention to each change in the response format.

Name _____ Date _____

Teacher _____ Grade _____

Denver Writing Attitude Survey

Make a circle around the answer that is most true for you.

How often do you do each of the following things?

	Almost every day	Once or twice a week	Once or twice a month	A few times a year	Never or hardly ever
1. Write letters *at home* to friends or relatives.	A	B	C	D	E
2. Write notes and personal messages at school or home.	A	B	C	D	E
3. Write stories, poems, or diaries that are *not schoolwork*.	A	B	C	D	E

4. What kind of writer do you think you are?

    A. A very good writer.

    B. A good writer.

    C. An average writer.

    D. A poor writer.

    E. A very poor writer.

(continued)

The following statements are true for some people. They may or may not be true for you, or they may be true for you only part of the time. How often is each of the following sentences true for you?

		Almost always	More than half the time	About half the time	Less than half the time	Never or hardly ever
5.	Other people like what I write.	A	B	C	D	E
6.	Writing helps me think more clearly.	A	B	C	D	E
7.	I feel proud of the things I write in school.	A	B	C	D	E
8.	Writing helps me tell others what I've learned.	A	B	C	D	E
9.	Writing helps me tell others how I feel about things.	A	B	C	D	E
10.	Writing helps me understand my own feelings about things.	A	B	C	D	E
11.	Writing helps me think about what I've learned.	A	B	C	D	E
12.	I am good at putting my ideas down on paper.	A	B	C	D	E

Denver Writing Attitude Survey by W. Alan Davis and Lynn K. Rhodes. Reprinted with permission of the authors.

Nombre _____ Grado _____

Maestro/a _____ Fecha _____

Encuesta Sobre Escritura de Denver

Encierre en un círculo la letra de la respuesta que sea más cierta para usted.

¿Con qué frecuencia hace lo siguiente?

		Casi cada día	Una o dos veces por semana	Una o dos veces al mes	Varias veces al año	Nunca o casi nunca
1.	Escribir cartas, *en casa*, en la casa a amigos o familiares.	A	B	C	D	E
2.	Escribir notas o mensajes en la escuela o en su hogar.	A	B	C	D	E
3.	Escribir historias, poemas, o diarios *que no sean tarea escolar*.	A	B	C	D	E

4. ¿Qué tipo de escritor se considera usted?

    A. Excelente escritor.

    B. Buen escritor.

    C. Escritor regular.

    D. Escritor con problemas.

    E. Escritor con muchos problemas.

(continuado)

Las siguientes declaraciones son ciertas para alguna gente. Estas declaraciones no necesariamente son aplicables a usted, or serán ciertas solo en algunas ocaciones. ¿Con qué frecuencia es cada una de las siguientes declaraciones cierta para usted?

	Casi siempre	Más de la mitad del tiempo	Como mitad del tiempo	Menos de la mitad del tiempo	Nunca o casi nunca
5. A otra gente le gusta lo que escribo.	A	B	C	D	E
6. El escribir me ayuda a pensar más claramente.	A	B	C	D	E
7. Me siento orgulloso/a de lo que escribo en la escuela.	A	B	C	D	E
8. El escribir me ayuda para expresar a otras personas lo que he aprendido.	A	B	C	D	E
9. El escribir me ayuda a comunicar a otras personas cómo me hacen sentir ciertas cosas.	A	B	C	D	E
10. El escribir me ayuda a comprender mis sentimientos acerca de las cosas que me rodean.	A	B	C	D	E
11. El escribir me ayuda a pensar en lo que he aprendido.	A	B	C	D	E
12. Me considero hábil para escribir mis ideas.	A	B	C	D	E

Denver Writing Attitude Survey by W. Alan Davis and Lynn K. Rhodes. Reprinted with permission of the authors.

An Inventory of Classroom Writing Use

▨ Directions:

1. Fill out the information blanks at the top of the page for each student with whom you want to use this questionnaire.

2. For each question, indicate with a mark on the appropriate line the degree to which the student exhibits the described writing behaviors.

3. For each question, indicate with a check mark in the appropriate box whether the described writing is initiated by you or another teacher, by the student, or by both.

4. Fill out the questionnaire at intervals that you find helpful in planning instruction. It may be helpful to fill out this questionnaire approximately a month after the school year begins and about midway through the year in order to plan instruction. Or you may find it helpful to use the questionnaire toward the end of each grading period.

5. In addition to being useful for planning instruction, the questionnaire may also be useful in evaluating both the student's development as a lifelong writer and the effectiveness of your program's goals and activities.

There are a number of questions which can be asked on the basis of students' answers to this questionnaire that may lead you to consider the curriculum you are providing for students:

1. Are students having enough writing opportunities?

2. Are students writing about a wide range of topics?

3. Are students developing the skills necessary to choose and expand their own writing topics?

4. Are students finding writing an enjoyable part of their lives?

5. Do students consider writing meaningful and relevant to their lives?

6. Is the curriculum you have established conducive to the above goals? (Check "teacher-initiated" column)

7. Are students moving toward independence in relationship to the above goals? (Is there a change in scores over time? Is there a movement toward more "student-initiated" behaviors?)

8. Are the scores lower for low ability students? If so, is the curriculum you have established for the low ability students conducive to growth in the above goals?

9. Compare the data from several students whose scores are quite different and think about why they are different. What can you do to influence the situation?

Name _____   Grade _____

Teacher _____   Date _____

An Inventory of Classroom Writing Use

To what extent does the student:

	Not at all	A little	To some extent	To a large extent	To a great extent	Teacher-initiated	Student-initiated
1. Utilize available environmental print to support his or her writing?	A	B	C	D	E	☐	☐
2. Gather related information for a specific purpose from a variety of sources as a way of building background knowledge, confirming/clarifying ideas, etc. for writing tasks?	A	B	C	D	E	☐	☐
3. Engage in a wide variety of writing (e.g., topics, style genre, audience, etc.)?	A	B	C	D	E	☐	☐
4. Engage in writing at various difficulty levels based on topic and genre familiarity, challenge of task, etc.?	A	B	C	D	E	☐	☐
5. Choose to share writing with peers, family, teacher, etc.?	A	B	C	D	E	☐	☐
6. Engage in meaningful revision and editing of his or her draft writing?	A	B	C	D	E	☐	☐
7. Choose to write during "choice" time?	A	B	C	D	E	☐	☐
8. Engage fully in writing during sustained silent writing periods?	A	B	C	D	E	☐	☐
9. Attend to writer's choices/ styles when discussing reading experiences?	A	B	C	D	E	☐	☐

An Inventory of Classroom Writing Use adapted by Lori L. Conrad. Reprinted with permission of the author.

The Authoring Cycle Profile

The purpose of *The Authoring Cycle Profile* is to assess the writing process, in addition to the finished product, in an organized way. The profile reflects areas of the authoring cycle as described by Harste, Short, and Burke (1988). The profile was developed by Nancy L. Shanklin.

The Authoring Cycle Profile may be used to observe the writing process of one to six students at a time. It takes approximately 40 minutes over three days to collect information: Day 1, rehearse and draft; Day 2, Authors' Circle; Day 3, revise and edit. Other ways to divide the time are also possible; the profile is flexible in this regard. Page 76 outlines a plan for assessing an entire class using *The Authoring Cycle Profile* over a period of seven days.

The profile consists of several pages linked to phases of the authoring cycle. It is designed so that information can be gathered on a single set of forms for up to six students at a time. Behaviors are listed at the top of each page; the behaviors are those that proficient writers tend to use during that part of the writing process. These lists are meant to suggest behaviors that teachers may want to look for. They are *not* meant to be totally inclusive, and a teacher will probably observe additional behaviors that he or she will want to note. The codes for the listed behaviors can also be used as a way to help the teacher save time while taking his or her own observational notes. The first page is used to record behaviors related to students' rehearsal for writing. The second page is for notes considering the strategies students use for drafting. The third page is to record students' behavior in Authors' Circle or during teacher-student or peer-response groups. The fourth page is for anecdotal notes concerning students' revisions, and the fifth page is for recording editing strategies. While the form may at first seem to make the steps of the writing process too discrete, it does allow teachers to make notes on some students' recursive use of the various parts of the writing process.

Following this in-depth examination of students' writing processes, the sixth page of *The Authoring Cycle Profile* guides the teacher's assessments of students' final written products. The last page is a summary sheet teachers can use for reflecting upon students' strengths and weaknesses and for planning instruction. The profile is designed so that notes about the six students can be cut apart and placed in students' individual writing folders or portfolios following the assessment.

We prefer using the instrument to guide our observations of students' writing, and do not attach scores. However, if this is useful or desirable, ratings can be generated from *The Authoring Cycle Profile*. If used for rating, teachers need to understand that the scheme used in the profile is basically analytic. The teacher rates a student's behaviors 1 to 5 for each area. The exact meaning of the 1 to 5 would be determined by exemplars from an entire set of writing samples. If a teacher is using the profile only in his or her own classroom, he or she should be consistent from one use to the next. A teacher might want to use the profile with children two or three times per year.

References

Harste, J., K. Short., & C. Burke (1988). *Creating classrooms for authors.* Portsmouth, NH: Heinemann.

Directions

1. Arrange the students (1 to 6) in a group so that you can observe each of them easily.

Day 1

2. Tell the students that they will do some writing today and that you will give them a few minutes to think and then to write down some topics they might write about. Ask each student to share one or two topics he or she may choose to write about. Because of time constraints do not encourage students to elaborate on their topics.

3. If students are not able to generate their own topics, suggest that you would like them to write true stories about themselves. (You may add, "So I can get to know you better.")

4. Suggest to students that they may want to draw a picture or do other things that help them gather ideas for writing. When the students are ready to do so, they may begin drafting their pieces.

5. Take anecdotal notes on the "Rehearsing and Drafting" pages of the profile as children move through the writing process. You can use the items at the top of each page to guide your thinking about this part of the process. You can also use the letter given to each behavior as a way to save time in note taking. If you are doing an individual assessment, it often works best if you also draw and write like the students while you take notes about what the student is doing and saying.

6. After each student has finished with his or her piece, ask him or her to read it to you. If you are working with only one student, read your piece too.

■ Day 2

7. The following day, review Authors' Circle procedures (see Harste, Short & Burke, 1988, pp. 221–226). Then have the students share their pieces in the Authors' Circle. Before the Authors' Circle, ask students if they want to reread and do any revising or editing. Record notes on the "Conferring/Authors' Circle" page of the profile.

■ Day 3

8. The following day, allow students time to revise and edit their pieces. Make your observations of their revision and editing processes on the "Revising" and "Editing" pages of the profile.

9. Collect final pieces and assess them for message, form, and conventions, recording information in the "Assessment of Final Product" page of the profile.

10. Use the "Summary and Instructional Recommendations" page to help you plan further instruction for students.

■ Notes

1. Ratings can be given to students for each part of the process if this is desired, but it is not necessary. The more valuable assessment information is the anecdotal notes that you take; it is these that will help you most in planning instruction.

2. See the "Plan for Class Assessment" on the next page for ideas about how to give *The Authoring Cycle Profile* to an entire class over a period of seven days.

Authoring Cycle Profile by Nancy L. Shanklin. Reprinted with permission of the author.

Authoring Cycle Profile
Plan for Class Assessment

	Monday	Tuesday	Wednesday	Thursday	Friday
20–40 minutes	Group 1 Rehearse & draft	Group 2 Rehearse & draft	Group 3 Rehearse & draft	Group 4 Rehearse & draft	Group 5 Rehearse & draft
15–20 minutes		Group 1 Share Authors' Circle	Group 1 Revise & edit	Group 2 Revise & edit	Group 3 Revise & edit
15–20 minutes			Group 2 Share Authors' Circle	Group 3 Share Authors' Circle	Group 4 Share Authors' Circle
20–40 minutes					
15–20 minutes	Group 4 Revise & edit	Group 5 Revise & edit			
15–20 minutes	Group 5 Share Authors' Circle				

Notes:

1. All students in the class are to participate in the Authors' Circle. The group listed each day is to share writing.

2. During the time the assigned group is rehearsing and drafting other students can be engaged in silent reading or other activities, such as being read to by another adult, watching filmstrips or videos on authors or books, or completing other projects.

3. During the time the assigned group is revising and editing, other students can be writing and sharing learning log entries about what they have been reading.

4. We suggest that the teacher rate the final products and make instructional recommendations as each group finishes. That way the workload seems more manageably spaced.

I. Rehearsing

A. Consults personal topics list.
B. Uses background knowledge.
C. Uses personal experiences.
D. Sketches to get ideas.
E. Webs/makes jot list.
F. Takes time to ponder task, topic, etc.

G. Borrows ideas from books, movies.
H. Talks to peers/teacher.
I. Chooses from among teacher suggestions.
J. Has authentic purpose and audience in mind.
K. Positive attitude toward writing.

Name	Rating (1–5)	Comments
1. _____	_____	_____
		_____
		_____
		_____
2. _____	_____	_____
		_____
		_____
		_____
3. _____	_____	_____
		_____
		_____
		_____
4. _____	_____	_____
		_____
		_____
		_____
5. _____	_____	_____
		_____
		_____
		_____
6. _____	_____	_____
		_____
		_____
		_____

II. Drafting

A. Fluent in getting ideas down.
B. Rereads while drafting.
C. Text makes sense.

Spelling:
D. Risks spelling new words.

E. Writes down sounds heard.
F. Applies knowledge of spelling rules.
G. Thinks of derivation.
H. Consults another source: library book, environment, dictionary.
I. Asks teacher or peer for spelling.

Name	Rating (1–5)	Comments
1. _____	_____	_____
Fluency, etc.	_____	_____
Spelling	_____	_____
		_____
2. _____	_____	_____
Fluency, etc.	_____	_____
Spelling	_____	_____
		_____
3. _____	_____	_____
Fluency, etc.	_____	_____
Spelling	_____	_____
		_____
4. _____	_____	_____
Fluency, etc.	_____	_____
Spelling	_____	_____
		_____
5. _____	_____	_____
Fluency, etc.	_____	_____
Spelling	_____	_____
		_____
6. _____	_____	_____
Fluency, etc.	_____	_____
Spelling	_____	_____
		_____

III. Conferring/Authors' Circle

A. Can read writing back.
B. Text makes sense.
C. Willingly shares and discusses own writing.
D. Listens actively.

E. Makes notes of questions, ideas, etc., to include in revisions.
F. Makes good suggestions to other writers.

Name	Rating (1–5)	Comments
1.		
2.		
3.		
4.		
5.		
6.		

IV. Revising

A. Makes sense/clarifies content.
B. Addresses questions from conferring with self.
C. Addresses questions from conferring with others.

D. Level of revision: word, sentence, larger.
E. Elaborates (may use carets).
F. Deletes (may cross out).
G. Reorganizes (may use arrows).

Name	Rating (1–5)	Comments
1. _____	_____	_____
		_____
		_____
		_____
2. _____	_____	_____
		_____
		_____
		_____
3. _____	_____	_____
		_____
		_____
		_____
4. _____	_____	_____
		_____
		_____
		_____
5. _____	_____	_____
		_____
		_____
		_____
6. _____	_____	_____
		_____
		_____
		_____

Writing

V. Editing

A. Attends to grammar/usage.
B. Attends to capitalization.
C. Attends to punctuation.
D. Attends to paragraphing, other elements of form.

E. Is able to detect spelling errors.
F. Writes word several times to determine correct spelling.
G. Checks another source or the dictionary.

Name	Rating (1–5)	Comments
1.		
2.		
3.		
4.		
5.		
6.		

VI. Assessment of Final Product

Message/Function (1-5) x 2

Communicates clearly.
Well developed.
Sense of voice.
Vocabulary appropriate to
    topic.
Sense of Audience.

Structure (1-5)

Appropriate to content.
Well organized.
Variety of sentence
    structures.
Use of transitions.

Conventions (1-5)

Correct spelling.
Appropriate usage.
Capitalization.
Punctuation.
Manuscript.

Name	Rating (1–5)	Comments
1. _____	_____	_____
Message (x 2)	_____	_____
Structure.	_____	_____
Conventions	_____	_____
2. _____	_____	_____
Message (x 2)	_____	_____
Structure.	_____	_____
Conventions	_____	_____
3. _____	_____	_____
Message (x 2)	_____	_____
Structure.	_____	_____
Conventions	_____	_____
4. _____	_____	_____
Message (x 2)	_____	_____
Structure.	_____	_____
Conventions	_____	_____
5. _____	_____	_____
Message (x 2)	_____	_____
Structure.	_____	_____
Conventions	_____	_____
6. _____	_____	_____
Message (x 2)	_____	_____
Structure.	_____	_____
Conventions	_____	_____

VII. Summary and Instructional Recommendations

Name   Total Rating   Instructional recommendations:

1. _____ _____

    Strengths: _____

    _____

    Areas of development: _____

    _____

2. _____ _____

    Strengths: _____

    _____

    Areas of development: _____

    _____

3. _____ _____

    Strengths: _____

    _____

    Areas of development: _____

    _____

4. _____ _____

    Strengths: _____

    _____

    Areas of development: _____

    _____

5. _____ _____

    Strengths: _____

    _____

    Areas of development: _____

    _____

6. _____ _____

    Strengths: _____

    _____

    Areas of development: _____

    _____

Developed by Nancy L. Shanklin. Reprinted with permission of the author.

Spelling Analysis

References for Spelling Analysis
Spelling Concepts and Attitudes
My Strategies for Spelling

Analysis of spelling miscues or unconventional spelling provides teachers with information about students' spelling development and strategies. An analysis of a student's spellings allows the teacher to determine what orthographic information the child uses to generate spellings of words. Observing the student's writing process yields information about the strategies the student uses to spell words.

Spelling development is most often defined in terms of spelling "stages." For theoretical reasons we prefer to consider spelling development as a continuum and these "stages" simply as developmental points along the continuum. Although various researchers and educators use different terminology for these developmental points, the definitions are similar from one researcher to another. The labels do not matter. What matters is your understanding of how spelling changes over time.

In this section, we provide a list of books and articles that contain procedures for analyzing student spelling. The analyses result in either the identification of a point along the spelling development continuum that best represents the kinds of spellings the student currently produces or a description of the spelling strategies the student uses. For each reference, the terminology used by the researcher is provided along with a description of the procedures.

This section also contains a series of interview questions about spelling, *Spelling Concepts and Attitudes*, suggested by Sandra Wilde (1992, p. 164). The questions are designed to explore students' perceptions of spelling and their spelling strategies.

Finally, the section contains a spelling strategies Lickert scale, *My Strategies for Spelling*, developed by Nancy Shanklin. The scale is intended to reveal how students approach spelling in both drafting and editing.

The sections of this handbook entitled "Self-Assessments of Writing," "Ongoing Observations of Writing," and "Literacy at Home" also include various instruments for assessing students' spelling development and strategy use.

Reference

Wilde, S. 1992. *You kan red this!* Portsmouth, NH: Heinemann.

References for Spelling Analysis

Bean, W., & C. Bouffler (1987). *Spell by writing.* Portsmouth, NH: Heinemann.

The authors state: "Invented spelling is not a stage but a strategy used by all writers" (p. 16). Ten strategies used to generate spellings are listed; they can be assessed through observation. The strategies are:

- Spelling as it sounds.

- Spelling as it sounds out.

- Spelling as it articulates.

- Spelling as it means.

- Spelling as it looks.

- Spelling by analogy.

- Spelling by linguistic context.

- Spelling by reference to an authority.

- Opting for an alternative structure.

- Spelling by being indeterminate.

Buchanan, E. (1989). *Spelling for whole language classrooms.* New York: Richard C. Owen.

Buchanan labels the spelling "stages" as prephonetic, early phonetic, advanced phonetic, phonic, and syntactic-semantic.

To assess spelling, Buchanan recommends analyzing the spellings in a writing sample. Each word is listed on a form (see p. 104 of the book) and then coded according to one or more of the following categories:

- Phonetic: the misspelling is phonetic.

- Phonic: the misspelling is related to using phonic cues.

- Homophone: the student used the wrong form of a homophone.

- Suffix: a suffix is misspelled, misused, or omitted.

- Root: the root of a word is misspelled.

- Pronunciation: the misspelling has to do with pronunciation.

- Standard spelling: word is spelled correctly.

- Penmanship: the apparent misspelling is due to penmanship.

Gentry, R. J. (1985). You can analyze developmental spelling—and here's how to do it! *Early Years: K–8*, May, 44–45.

Gentry labels the spelling "stages" as precommunicative, semiphonetic, phonetic, transitional, and correct.

To assess spelling, the author lists ten words and recommends giving them to K–2 students. Each word is labeled according to the stage the spelling best represents. The child's probable developmental level is determined by the stage that is characterized by most of the spellings.

Sharp, Q. Q. (1989). *Evaluation: Whole language checklists for evaluating your children*. New York: Scholastic.

Sharp (pgs. 18-19) recommends that students retell a story in writing and that this writing can be used to figure a percentage of invented spelling and conventional spelling in the retelling. If the students periodically retell the same story in writing, the progress of students in moving toward conventional spelling may be analyzed.

Temple, C., R. Nathan, N. Burris, & F. Temple (1988). *The beginnings of writing*. Boston: Allyn & Bacon.

The authors label the spelling "stages" as prephonemic, early phonemic, letter-name, transitional, and correct.

To assess spelling, the authors recommend analyzing the spellings contained in writing samples or spellings from a word list included in the book (pp. 106–107). Scoring the student's spelling is a matter of deciding which category the spelling of each word falls into:

0: if spelling of word is prephonemic.

1: if spelling of word is early phonemic.

2: if spelling of word is letter-name.

3: if spelling of word is transitional.

4: if spelling of word is correct.

After scoring each word, figure both the average and the mode in order to determine what "stage" most of the student's spellings fall into.

Wilde, S. (1989). Looking at invented spelling: A kidwatcher's guide to spelling, Part I. In K. S. Goodman, Y. M. Goodman, & W. J. Hood (Eds.), *The whole language evaluation book*, pp. 213–226. Portsmouth, NH: Heinemann.

Wilde proposes eight questions for analyzing children's spellings:

1. Is the spelling an unusual one?

2. Does the spelling represent consonants nonconventionally?

3. Does the spelling represent vowels nonconventionally?

4. Does the spelling use suffixes nonconventionally?

5. Is the invented spelling a permutation of the intended word?

6. Does the invented spelling differ from the conventional one by only a single letter?

7. Is the invented spelling a real word?

8. Are the invented and conventional spellings punctuated differently?

Using the first ten or so invented spellings from a writing sample, code each spelling for the eight questions and then figure the total for each code.

Wilde, S. (1989). Understanding spelling strategies: A kidwatcher's guide to spelling, Part II. In K. S. Goodman, Y. M. Goodman, & W. J. Hood (Eds.), *The whole language evaluation book*, pp. 227–236. Portsmouth, NH: Heinemann.

Wilde recommends observing students during the writing process to record evidence of five spelling strategies:

1. Placeholder spelling strategy: "I just wrote it any way."

2. Human resource spelling strategy: "How do you spell *people*?"

3. Textual resource spelling strategy: "I need the dictionary."

4. Generation, monitoring, and revision strategy: "Say is *s-a-y*, huh?"

5. Ownership strategy: "I know how to spell *rodeo*."

Wilde, S. (1992). *You kan red this!* Portsmouth, NH: Heinemann.

Although this book focuses on instruction in spelling and punctuation, one chapter is devoted to the evaluation of spelling, and other useful information is sprinkled throughout the book. Especially good is the discussion of grading and the metacognitive interview (p. 164), also by Wilde, on the next page of this handbook.

Name _____   Date _____

Spelling Concepts and Attitudes

1. Is spelling important? Why?

   _____

   _____

2. How do you feel about spelling? Do you like trying to figure out how to spell words?

   _____

3. When is it important to spell correctly?

   _____

   _____

4. Who's a good speller that you know? What makes him/her a good speller? Does he/she ever make a spelling mistake?

   _____

   _____

5. How do people learn how to spell? How did you learn how to spell? Are you still learning?

   _____

   _____

6. Why do you think words are spelled the way they are?

   _____

   _____

Spelling Strategies

7. What do you do when you don't know how to spell a word?

   _____

   _____

8. What else could you do?

_____

_____

9. Where in the classroom would you look if you wanted to find how to spell a word?

_____

_____

10. If you were at home, where would you look?

_____

_____

11. How do you know when you've spelled something right?

_____

_____

12. What do you do when you haven't spelled something right?

_____

_____

Questions about Specific Spellings

13. How did you figure out how to spell this word?

_____

_____

14. Why did you change this spelling?

_____

_____

15. Pick out some words that you think are spelled wrong. Tell/show me how you could change them to the right spelling.

_____

_____

Spelling Concepts and Attitudes reprinted with permission of Sandra Wilde: *You Kan Red This!* (Heinemann Educational Books, Portsmouth, NH, 1992)

Name _____   Date _____

Teacher _____   Grade _____

My Strategies for Spelling

	Often	Sometimes	Almost Never	Never
During drafting . . .				
I write down the sounds I hear and keep going.	4	3	2	1
I write down what I think the word looks like and keep going.	4	3	2	1
I mark any word that doesn't look right and keep going.	4	3	2	1
I look around the room to see if the word is on a sign, bulletin board, chart, or somewhere else.	4	3	2	1
I look for the word in a book other than a dictionary.	4	3	2	1
I think about the parts of the word.	4	3	2	1
I think of other words I know how to spell that may be similar to the word I want to spell.	4	3	2	1
I think about the spelling rules I know.	4	3	2	1
During editing . . .				
I try to spell the word several different ways and pick the one that looks right.	4	3	2	1
I look in the dictionary.	4	3	2	1
I ask someone.	4	3	2	1
I know I'll use the word again so I put it on my personal spelling list.	4	3	2	1

Other strategies I use for spelling are:

_____

_____

_____

My Strategies for Spelling by Nancy L. Shanklin. Reprinted with permission of author.

Self-Assessments of Writing

Writing Workshop
Challenging Myself as a Writer
Authors' Circle
Revising Writing
Strong Verbs
Spelling Strategies
Spelling Progress
What I Do Well in Writing/What I'm Working on in Writing
Researching and Report Writing
Six-Week Student Assessment

The self-assessments that follow are only a few of those that teachers have used successfully to engage students in considering what they are learning and what they are responsible for as writers. Like every other form of assessment teachers use, these were designed to directly reflect and gauge the impact of instruction on students' writing.

Self-assessments have two purposes. First, they provide a way for the teacher to encourage the student to become responsible for what has been taught and what is expected of him or her as a result. Second, the students' responses provide rich data for the teacher in determining the next steps in instructional planning. They reveal students' understanding of what the teacher has taught and often provide hints about what else needs to be taught.

Some of the self-assessments are analogous versions of the teacher observation forms presented in the next section. Involving both teacher and student in assessing the same aspect of writing results in data from two points of view. Often the student's and teacher's data corroborate one another, but when they do not, the teacher can see that the student may not be learning or may be learning something different from what the teacher intended or assumed.

You will notice that the self-assessments tend to be quite short. In most cases, we suggest keeping them to half a page with no more than three questions (fewer if possible). When there is more than a single question, the questions usually focus on the same aspect of writing, asking the student to look at it from different angles.

Other examples of self-assessment may be found in *Windows Into Literacy.*

Writing Workshop

1. How much time did you spend writing during Writing Workshop today?

   all the time   most of the time   some of the time   not at all

2. If you didn't spend all your time writing, why didn't you?

   _____

   _____

3. What will help you so that you'll spend all your time writing during the next Writing Workshop?

   _____

   _____

Cut here--

Name _____   Date _____

Title or topic _____

Challenging Myself as a Writer

1. Is the piece I am writing challenging me to be a better writer?

   Yes   Sort of   No

2. Why?

   _____

   _____

   _____

   _____

   _____

Name _____ Date _____

Title or topic _____

Authors' Circle

1. Did you use all the steps for Authors' Circle? Write yes or no in each blank.
    - Read my piece to the group. _____
    - Asked someone to tell what they heard. _____
    - Asked several people to tell what they liked. _____
    - Asked if there were suggestions. _____
    - Thanked the group for their help. _____
    - Thought about the suggestions back at my desk. _____

2. What do you think you did especially well during Authors' Circle?

    _____

    _____

Cut here- -

Name _____ Date _____

Authors' Circle

1. How much did you participate in Authors' Circle today?

    about the right amount   too much   too little   not at all

2. What was an important contribution you made during Authors' Circle?

    _____

    _____

3. What was an important contribution made by someone else in the group? (Identify the person and tell what he or she said.)

    _____

    _____

Name _____

Name of your piece _____

Revising Writing

Inside the appropriate pencil, record the revisions you made in your writing.

1. Rereading   Date _____

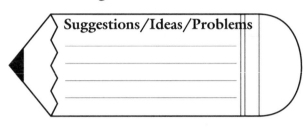 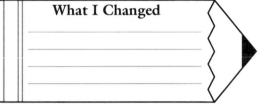

2. Peer Conference   Date _____

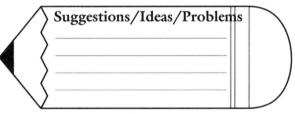 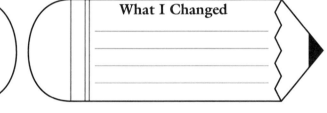

3. Authors' Circle   Date _____

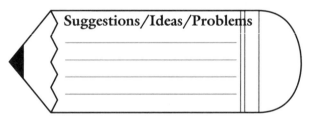 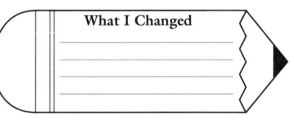

4. Teacher Conference   Date _____

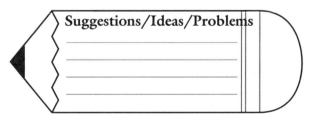 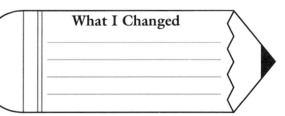

Revising Writing by Shari Steele-Schreiber. Reprinted with permission of the author.

Name _____ Date _____

Title of your piece _____

Revising Writing

In Authors' Circle today, your classmates gave you several suggestions about things that might make your piece better.

In the space below, write down one suggestion that you plan to use in revising your piece. Tell why.

_____

_____

_____

In the space below, write down one suggestion that you don't plan to use in revising your piece. Tell why.

_____

_____

_____

Cut here--

Name _____ Date _____

Title or topic _____

Strong Verbs

1. For the last week we have been working on using strong verbs in our writing. How did you do with that while you were writing today?

_____

_____

2. Give an example of a sentence from your writing in which you used a strong verb. Copy the sentence in the space below and underline the strong verb.

_____

_____

Name _____ Date _____

Title or topic _____

Spelling Strategies

Circle one: I am writing a first draft.

I am revising.

I am editing.

What strategies did you use to spell difficult words as you were writing today?
(Underline any strategies you used. Star the strategies you used a lot.)

- Thought about how the word should look.
- Sounded the word out.
- Marked words that didn't look right and kept writing.
- Thought about the parts of the word.
- Wrote the word several different ways and chose the one that looked best.
- Thought about other words that were like the difficult word.
- Looked up the word in the dictionary.
- Asked someone how to spell the word.

Cut here- -

Name _____ Date _____

Spelling Progress

How has your spelling improved in the last _____ weeks?

_____

_____

_____

_____

What do you need to work on in your spelling?

_____

_____

_____

_____

Name _____

What I Do Well in Writing

Date	

What I'm Working on in Writing

Date	

Name _____ Date _____

Title of report _____

Researching and Report Writing

1. How did this assignment make you feel about yourself as a researcher? Why?

    _____

    _____

    _____

2. At what stage did you feel most confident in your research? Why?

    _____

    _____

    _____

3. What did you do well in writing your report?

    _____

    _____

    _____

4. What would you like to do better or differently the next time you do research and write a report?

    _____

    _____

    _____

5. What do you think I need to teach or show you to make research and writing a report easier for you next time?

    _____

    _____

    _____

Adapted by Maureen Holland, Douglas County, CO, Public Schools. From Gawith, G. 1987: *Information alive: Information skills for research and reading,*. Auckland, New Zealand: Longman Paul.

Name _____ Date _____

Six-Week Student Assessment

1. When you are evaluating my writing, I would like you to look most carefully at the following piece(s) of writing, which I consider to be my best for this six weeks:

   _____

   _____

   _____

2. I think that the above piece(s) of writing is (are) my best effort this six weeks because:

   _____

   _____

   _____

3. In my writing during the last six weeks, I have worked the hardest on:

   _____

   _____

   _____

Writing Workshop Performance

Circle the appropriate letter for each item below. (G equals GOOD EFFORT and N equals NEED TO WORK HARDER ON THIS.)

1. Writing folder upkeep (Use of goal-setting   G   N
   calendar, class note taking, upkeep of skills
   and spelling list, keeping well-organized
   collection of all drafts).

2. Use of writing process (Evidence of revision,   G   N
   conferring, editing).

(continued)

3. Amount of writing done.   G   N

4. Amount of writing finalized.   G   N

5. Trying new types of writing.   G   N

6. On-task behavior during Writing Workshop.   G   N

7. Six week goal(s) accomplished.   G   N

Based on the above assessment, I believe that my overall writing grade for this six weeks should be:

My writing goal for the coming six weeks is

_____

_____

_____

_____

_____

_____

_____

_____

_____

_____

_____

_____

_____

_____

_____

Ongoing Observations of Writing

Writing Workshop
Writing Conference
Authors' Circle
Spelling Strategies
Spelling
Observations of Authoring Cycle
Six-Week Assessment

The observation forms that follow are designed for teachers to use as students are involved in regular ongoing classroom activities. You don't need to ask the students to do anything different from what they usually do in order to make the observations.

The forms are analogous to those provided as examples in the "Self-Evaluations in Writing" section that precedes this. Observations made by the teacher can be used to corroborate what students perceive and observe about themselves in self-assessments. The forms are examples only; you will be able to think of others that guide your thinking and inform your instruction more effectively and to adapt those included here.

Like the self-evaluations, the observation forms focus on the collection of only a small portion of the potential data that might be recorded. Most teachers find that their observations are sharper if they don't try to observe too many aspects of writing at once. If you use such observation forms and change them frequently, you can still collect the wide range of data you are interested in over time.

The form called *Observations of Authoring Cycle,* designed by Nancy Shanklin, can be used during any phase of the authoring cycle that you want to collect information about: rehearsing, drafting, conferring or Authors' Circle, revising, editing, or publishing. The form included in this section focuses on the last four phases of the authoring cycle. You can write notes in any box for which you make observations about a child's piece of writing; each note should be dated so that the pacing of a child's work may also be analyzed.

The final assessment form in this section, *Six-Week Assessment,* was designed by Judith M. Jindrich of the Littleton, Colorado, Public Schools for use with her middle school students. Jindrich uses the form in conjunction with the self-assessment form in the previous section in order to arrive at a grade and to do some thinking about what each student's goal should be for the following grading term. If the student's assessment or goal is quite different from her assessment or goal, Jindrich confers with the student in order to better communicate her expectations and values about writing and understand the student's expectations and values.

Name _____ Date _____ No. Minutes _____

Writing Workshop

1. How much time did the student spend writing during Writing Workshop today?

    all the time   most of the time   some of the time   not at all

2. If not all of the time, what appeared to be the source of difficulty?

    _____

    _____

    _____

    _____

3. Source of difficulty determined through: observation   interview

Cut here -

Name _____ Date _____

Title or topic_____

Writing Conference

1. Was the student ready for his or her writing conference today? (If not, how was he or she not ready?)

    _____

2. What did the student want help with during the conference?

    _____

3. What suggestions were made about the student's writing?

    _____

4. What did the student intend to do next as a result of the conference?

    _____

Date _____

Authors' Circle

1. What parts of the Authors' Circle went well? (When possible, note specific things done/said by students.)

    _____

    _____

    _____

2. What needs to be brought to the group's attention that would make Authors' Circle more effective?

    _____

    _____

    _____

Cut here- -

Date _____

Authors' Circle

List who made important contributions during Authors' Circle and what the contributions were:

Name	Contribution
_____	_____
_____	_____
_____	_____
_____	_____
_____	_____
_____	_____

Name _____ Date _____

Spelling Strategies

1. Circle what denotes the writing student is doing:

   drafting   revising   editing

2. What spelling strategies does the student appear to be using?

   _____

   _____

3. What spelling strategies need to be worked on?

   _____

   _____

   _____

Cut here---

Name _____ Date _____

Spelling

1. Circle what denotes the writing student is doing:

   drafting   revising   editing

2. What words is the student misspelling?

   _____

   _____

3. What are some possible reasons the misspellings are occurring?

   _____

   _____

   _____

Name _____

Observations of Authoring Cycle

	Date:	Date:	Date:
Title of Piece			
Conferring/ Authors' Circle			
Revising			
Editing			
Publishing			

Name _____   Date _____

Six-Week Assessment

Comments about this six weeks' writing:

_____

_____

_____

_____

_____

_____

_____

_____

_____

_____

_____

_____

Writing Workshop Performance

Circle the appropriate letter for each item below. (G equals GOOD EFFORT and N equals NEED TO WORK HARDER ON THIS.)

1. Writing folder upkeep (Use of goal-setting   G   N
   calendar, class note taking, upkeep of
   skills and spelling list, keeping well-organized
   collection of all drafts).

2. Use of writing process (Evidence of   G   N
   revision, conferring, editing).

(continued)

3. Amount of writing done.　　　　　　　　　G　　　N

4. Amount of writing finalized.　　　　　　　G　　　N

5. Good writing ideas or trying new types
   of writing.　　　　　　　　　　　　　　　G　　　N

6. On-task behavior during writing workshop.　G　　　N

7. Six week goal(s) accomplished.　　　　　　G　　　N

Based on the above assessment as well as on your self-assessment, your overall writing grade for this six weeks will be:

A suggested writing goal for the coming six weeks is:

_____

_____

_____

_____

_____

_____

_____

_____

_____

_____

_____

_____

_____

_____

_____

_____

_____

Six-Week Assessment by Judith M. Jindrich. Reprinted with permission of the author.

3

Emergent
Reading and Writing

Emergent Reader and Writer Interview

The *Emergent Reader and Writer Interview* was developed by a group of Denver Public School Chapter I teachers who had used Burke's *Reading Interview* and a similar writing interview with their older students. Although they found the original interviews helpful in planning instruction for students who were reading, they did not find them helpful in planning instruction for emergent readers.

Like the interviews the teachers gave to the older Chapter I children, the *Emergent Reader and Writer Interview* has an open-ended format. It initially assumes that the young child is an independent reader or writer by saying, "Tell me what kinds of things you read and write." If the child claims that he or she cannot read and write, the teacher has recourse to a set of questions (on the right side of the interview) that provides information helpful in planning instruction. If the child names things that he or she can read or write, the questions on the left side of the column are asked instead.

Emergent Reader and Writer Interview by Instructional Assistance Project teachers Denver, Colorado. Reprinted by permission of Patricia Fernquist, Instructional Assistance Project Teacher Representative.

Emergent Reading and Writing

Name _____   Date _____

Teacher _____   Grade _____

Emergent Reader and Writer Interview

1. Tell me what kinds of things you read.

   If positive response:

   Do you read (whatever child has mentioned) by yourself? (If no: Who helps?)

   _____

   _____

   _____

   _____

   Do you like to read? Why?

   _____

   _____

   _____

   _____

   Do you think you're a good reader? Why?

   _____

   _____

   _____

   _____

   _____

   If negative response:

   Are you learning to read?

   _____

   If yes: How are you learning to read and who is helping?

   _____

   _____

   _____

   Do you like to read? Why?

   _____

   _____

   If no: How do you think you'll learn to read and who do you think will help?

   _____

   _____

   _____

   Do you want to learn to read? Why?

   _____

   _____

   _____

2. Who reads to you? *or* Who reads to you besides (whomever the child has named previously)?

   _____

   _____

3. Tell me what kinds of things you write.

If positive response:	*If negative response:*
Do you write (whatever child has mentioned) by yourself? (If no: Who helps?)	Are you learning to write?
_____	_____
	If yes: How are you learning to write and who is helping?
	_____
Do you like to write? Why?	Do you like to write? Why?
_____	_____
	If no: How do you think you'll learn to write and who do you think will help?
	_____
Do you think you're a good writer? Why?	
_____	Do you want learn to write? Why?
	_____

4. Other information of interest:

_____

_____

_____

_____

_____

Emergent Reader and Writer Interview by Instructional Assistance Project teachers Denver, Colorado. Reprinted by permission of Patricia Fernquist, Instructional Assistance Project Teacher Representative.

Emergent Reading and Writing Evaluation

The *Emergent Reading and Writing Evaluation* was developed in response to the need for an instrument that would help Chapter I teachers in Denver Public Schools systematically observe students for whom miscue analysis was not yet appropriate.

Since the activities the students engage in during this assessment are all things that teachers could do instructionally in order to help students progress as readers and writers, many teachers new to emergent reading and writing instruction learn how to conduct such activities by using the instrument. In addition, because the descriptors are listed developmentally, teachers learn not only what to look for as they observe students' reading and writing, but also the developmental patterns they are likely to see as the children progress.

Use in Chapter I and Special Education

Early in the school year, Chapter I and Special Education teachers can utilize this instrument in order to assess any students, no matter what their age, who do not yet independently read unfamiliar text. Many teachers do the drawing and writing portions of the assessment in small groups and the remainder of the assessment individually. On the basis of assessment data they collect from administering the *Emergent Reading and Writing Evaluation* in the initial weeks of school, teachers can write initial educational plans for the students.

Although teachers need only mark the appropriate descriptors, it is also possible to numerically key each descriptor and thus to statistically analyze data. When students are post-tested on this instrument, the pre-post data are helpful in several ways. First, teachers can examine the progress of individual children and consider future instructional plans for them. Second, if the data are aggregated, it may be used to determine the successes and difficulties that individual teachers and groups of teachers have in emergent reading instruction; this information is very helpful in planning staff development specifically geared to teachers' needs.

Of course, it is inappropriate to use this assessment at the end of the school year as a post-test for children who are reading; a "ceiling effect" will result. For the sake of pre-post comparison, children who are reading at the end of the year are treated separately; their pretest scores on the *Emergent Reading and Writing Evaluation* are reported alongside the level of reading they are doing for the post-test miscue analysis.

Use in Regular Classrooms

The *Emergent Reading and Writing Evaluation* is useful to regular classroom teachers as well. Although some kindergarten and first-grade teachers use the instrument with each of their students, most use it to assess their least effective readers in order to gain more specific information about how to focus their instruction. Since the instrument is so helpful in monitoring the effect of instruction and planning next steps, some teachers administer the instrument to the same children after several months of instruction. This helps them to confirm their observations of children's progress and determine the focus of future instruction.

Validity and Reliability

The validity and content reliability of the *Emergent Reading and Writing Evaluation* was ascertained on a population of 129 Denver Public School kindergarten and first-grade children who were emergent readers. It was concluded that the instrument was a reliable and valid measure of emergent literacy development. For more information, see Jones (1989).

Reference

Jones, M. E. (1989). The Emergent Reading and Writing Evaluation: A Reliability and Content Validity Study. Ph.D. diss., University of Northern Colorado.

Emergent Reading and Writing Evaluation

Introduction

This instrument is designed to help teachers assess the literacy knowledge of children who are not yet reading unfamiliar text independently. The information gained from this instrument may be used by teachers to make decisions about literacy instruction. For that reason, the procedures are similar to everyday activities that students encounter in classrooms where teachers operate from a socio-psycholinguistic theoretical base. Children should be invited to participate in the evaluation activities in the same way they would be invited to participate in any other classroom activity. In no way should children be made to feel that they are being "tested" while participating in the *Emergent Reading and Writing Evaluation*. In fact, most of the tasks may be woven into everyday literacy instruction, including small group settings.

Since assessment should mirror classroom instruction, teachers who use this instrument should consider using only those parts that inform their instruction. Although the activities that are often found in whole language classrooms were kept in mind as this instrument was developed, it may be that some sections are not suitable for your students, that some sections or items require adaptation, or that some sections or items need to be added to better mirror the instruction experienced by children in your classroom. The sections included in this instrument are:

- Drawing
- Dictation
- First reading
- Second reading
- Familiarity with literature
- Book handling
- Reading a predictable book
- Retelling
- Writing

In addition, classroom teachers should determine whether it is necessary to use this instrument with all their students. It may be that it is most useful with those students who are finding that learning to read and write is a struggle.

This instrument was originally designed for a program that required a pre- and post-test of emergent readers/writers. It continues to be useful in such circumstances, but it may also be used far more flexibly. All the tasks will inform instruction no matter when children participate in them during the school year. There is no need to use the tasks in the sequence in which they are written here and, in fact, you may want to think about using some after the children have become more familiar with each other and with you.

The amount of time each task requires is variable and depends on the teacher and on the student being assessed. Time may not be as significant a factor if you regard each of the tasks as an opportunity for learning—for you and for the children.

Preparation

1. Read the procedures and decide which parts of the instrument you want to use. Decide which parts you will conduct individually and which in a group setting. In addition, decide which children you want to assess.

2. Review the materials that are required for each part of the instrument you have decided to use. Gather these so that they are readily available.

3. Review the descriptors for each section prior to administration in order to establish in your mind the types of behaviors you want to observe.

4. Establish a setting in which you can work with students individually or in small groups. The child's desk is fine; again, that setting is likely to be perceived as less test-like and more instructional.

5. Schedule sufficient time to assess the first student or two so that you can become more familiar with tasks and procedures as you work. Assessing the first student or two is likely to take more time than you estimate; don't rush yourself.

6. After you have assessed a student or two and have become more familiar with the tasks and procedures, reflect on the initial decisions you made about which students you wanted to assess, which tasks you wanted to use, and which you wanted to do individually or in small groups.

Administration

1. Explain to the child/children in simple terms what you will be doing. For example, you might say "We're going to spend some time together talking, drawing, writing, and reading." Again, be sure not to evoke a "testing" situation with your comments.

2. Make sure the child/children can see the print during all parts of the assessment.

Drawing

Materials:
- drawing paper
- crayons or markers
- pencil

The procedures may be adapted for a small group setting.

1. Tell the child to draw a picture of herself so that you can get to know more about her. Answer any questions the child may have about completing the task. You might want to tell the child that there will be a time limit to encourage her to work a little more quickly. If a child says she cannot draw herself, say something like, "Just do your best. I'll know it's you."

2. As the child works, take notes about what she is doing in her drawing, how she solves problems, what she talks about as she draws, etc. Write down anything that provides information about how the child approaches the task or about the child's language and social development.

    Try not to distract the child from drawing by talking with her, but do talk with her if she appears to require encouragement or further information. Do *not* make comments about the child's drawing (not even "You're doing a good job!"). If you do not understand something you see or observe, ask the child a quick question about it.

3. Ask the child to turn her drawing over to the other side and to write her first and last names on the paper. (If a child says she can't write, ask her to pretend to write the name.) When the child appears to be finished, say "Check your name and see if it's the way you want it."

    If a child writes her middle name instead of the last name or if the child doesn't write her last name, give some assistance. For example, you might say, "Yes, part of your name is "Anna" and you've written that. The other part is "Smith"; please write that part of your name too." Again, if the child says that she can't write the name, ask her to pretend to write it or to write it as well as she can.

    As the child writes, observe such things as:

    - use of capital and small letters.
    - letter and word reversal.
    - letter formation.

4. Review and clarify your notes about the child's drawing on the evaluation sheet under "Drawing" and mark the appropriate descriptors for "Drawing." Then mark the appropriate descriptors for "Name Writing" and record comments about the child's behavior.

▓ Dictation

Materials:
- medium point dark-colored marker
- wide-ruled paper
- drawing produced by child

1. Tell the child that you would like to get to know more about him. Produce the drawing the child did of himself and ask the child to tell you about himself. Say something like, "I'd like to know more about you. I plan to write down what you say." (If you also use this procedure as a post-test, decide on a general topic other than the one given here.)

2. As the child tells you about himself, print what the child says, angling the paper toward the child so that he can easily see you print the words. Use a medium point dark-colored marker and print large enough so that the print is easily visible. Space well between words. If you find that the printing is not readable for one reason or another, we recommend that you take a moment to recopy it. Remember, the child's reading performance is somewhat dependent on your printing! We find that wide-ruled paper used by adults works very well for this task if a space is left between each of the lines you print on; this kind of paper allows you to keep the dictation to one page.

3. As you print what the child says, say what you write as you write it.

4. If the child merely points at people or objects in the picture and labels them, respond by saying something like, "Yes, that's your bike. Tell me something about your bike." If the child's reply begins with a pronoun ("It's fun to ride."), put the child's label and sentence together. For example, print and say "My bike is fun to ride." If the child uses a dialect or less mature language patterns, preserve his language as you record what the child says. For example, if the child says, "Me and my brother gots a rabbit," print and read the child's language just that way.

5. Try to elicit at least three sentences but no more than five or six. If a child is very verbal, tell the child you only want to record a few very important things and let the child decide which ideas are most important.

6. As the child dictates the text, observe his pacing of the dictation. Does the child dictate a word at a time and watch you write it before giving you the next word? Does the child just keep giving you more ideas even though it is obvious you can't get them down fast enough? Does the child dictate a whole sentence or phrase and wait for you to finish writing and then add another sentence or phrase? Do you have to ask the child to slow down or speed up?

7. Also observe behavior that provides evidence of interest or lack of interest in print. For example, where is the child looking as you write the dictation? Is he

watching you commit the words to paper?   Does he make any comments or ask any questions about it? If the child is not watching you print the words, where is the child's visual attention?

8. Note any other interesting behavior that provides evidence of the child's language and social development.

9. Follow the dictation with an immediate "First Reading," using the procedures detailed in the next section.

10. After completing the "First Reading" procedures, mark the appropriate descriptors under "Dictation" on the evaluation sheet and record pertinent comments about the child's performance.

First Reading

Materials:
- dictation written by teacher
- dark-colored marker

1. When the child's dictation is complete, ask the child to read it aloud and point to the words as she does so.

    If the child tells you that she can't read what you've written, ask her to pretend to read. Be sure to remind the child to point as she reads or pretends to read.

2. Record the child's reading in the appropriate space on the evaluation sheet under "First Reading."   For the child who reads or restates the text so that it is quite similar to what she has dictated, jotting down miscues or differences between text and reading may be enough. For the child who reads the text quite differently from how she dictated it, write down (for your information, not to be shared with the child) what the child "reads."

3. As the child reads, observe the following behavior:

    - voice-print match (1-to-1 correspondence between saying a word and pointing to a word).
    - directionality (top to bottom, left to right).
    - confidence.
    - locus of visual attention.
    - other interesting behavior.

4. Ask the child some questions like the following to provide you with more information about her knowledge of print.

    - Point to where it says "bike."

- Point to where it says "red."
- Point to where it says "love."
- Find where it says "My dog's name is Scruffy."

In all, ask the child to find three words and one sentence.

5. Tell the child you want to keep her dictation as you print her name on the paper. Print the first and last names in upper- and lowercase letters (i.e., Anna Smith). Ask the child to read what you have just printed (her name). If she doesn't recognize her name, read it to her.

6. Ask the child to name any six letters in her name (first and last) as you point to the letters in random order. Circle those letters you asked the child to name and put a small mark above those letters the child names correctly.

7. On the basis of your observations in items 1-4, mark the appropriate descriptors under "First Reading" on the evaluation sheet and record pertinent comments about the child's performance. On the basis of your observations in items 5 and 6, mark the appropriate descriptors under "Name Reading" on the evaluation sheet and record pertinent comments about the child's performance.

Second Reading

Materials:
- dictation written by teacher
- copy of dictation

1. If the child seems to be using cues from the print during the "First Reading" procedures, ask the child to read the dictation again the following day.

2. At this second reading, have a second copy of the dictation available so that you can mark the child's miscues. If that is not possible, record as much information as you can about the child's reading just as you did on the previous day. See #3 under "First Reading" for behaviors to observe.

3. Mark the appropriate descriptors under "Second Reading" on the evaluation sheet and record pertinent comments about the child's performance.

Familiarity with Literature

Materials:

• Four folktales (see recommendations under #3 below)

1. Ask the child, "Do you know 'Mary Had a Little Lamb' or 'Jack and Jill' or 'Little Miss Muffett'?" (If child does not know them, try 'Humpty Dumpty,' 'Baa, Baa Black Sheep,' and 'Hickory Dickory Dock' in the same way.) If the child responds affirmatively about one or more of the rhymes, ask him to say the rhymes for you. If necessary, provide the first line to help the child get started.

2. Children may not be familiar with traditional folktales or nursery rhymes but may be familiar with other stories. In order to determine this, ask the child to name his favorite stories. Record the names of the stories mentioned for later reference. Ask the child to briefly tell you about them. It may be useful to note whether the stories are common to the child's cultural heritage and whether they were passed on via oral storytelling or in books.

3. Lay four traditional folktales on the table and ask the child, "Do you know any of these stories?" Let the child look through the books; the covers alone may not be sufficient for the child to recognize a story he knows. Ask the child to tell about each story he recognizes; a retelling of the story is not necessary because all you need to find out is whether the child really is familiar with one or more of the stories. This is usually easier to evaluate if the child does not page through the book as he tells about the story.

   For this task, we recommend that you use "The Three Little Pigs" and "The Three Bears" as well as two others from the following list (or similar folktales): "The Three Billy Goats Gruff," "Little Red Riding Hood," "Hansel and Gretel," "Jack and the Beanstalk," "The Bremen Town Musicians" and "The Little Red Hen."

4. Mark the appropriate descriptors under "Familiarity with Literature" and record pertinent information and comments about the child's performance. It might be very interesting for post-test comparision to keep a record of what folktales, rhymes, and stories the child knew at the beginning of the year.

Book Handling

Materials:
- *I Like Hats* by Blair Dawson (Scholastic, 1977) or another appropriate book

1. Use the book listed above or select another predictable book. If you choose a book other than the title listed, be sure it is suited to the various tasks in this section of the evaluation. (For a list of predictable books, see L. K. Rhodes, "I can read! Predictable books as resources for reading and writing instruction" in *Reading Teacher*, Feb. 1981.) Choose books with predictable language that are appropriate for normally achieving first graders to read on their own during the year. Consider not only the degree of predictability but also print size and number of words per page. In addition, try to choose books whose front cover is not reproduced on the back.

2. With the book in your hands, show the child the front cover and point to the title on the front cover of the book. Ask, "What is this?" or "What does this tell us?"

3. Read the book to the child without pointing and enjoy it together. If the child initiates conversation about any part of the book, interact in the way you normally would during a book reading. If the child attempts to read along with you, don't discourage her.

4. Tell the child you'd like to read the book again and encourage the child to read with you.

5. Hand the book to the child upside down and backwards. Say, "Open the book to the page where we should begin reading the story again." The child may open the book to either the title page or the first page of story; either is a fine place to begin reading.

6. If the child is unsuccessful, turn to the first page of the story. After inviting the child to read along, read the first four pages of the story while pointing to the words.

7. When you turn to page 5 ("I like divers' hats."), say to the child, "Show me with your finger exactly where I have to read now." Observe whether the child indicates the first word on the left-hand page.

8. Read this page of the book while pointing to the print, and then continue to read while pointing to words. If necessary, invite the child to read along again.

9. After reading page 10 ("and pirate hats. I like hats!"), tell the child: "Point to each word on this page and count as you go." If the child miscounts but almost gets it right, give her another chance by asking the same question for another page of text. (What the child needs to do here is indicate one-to-one correspondence between words and numbers. Do not conclude that the child does

not have the concept of "wordness" if she leaves out a number during counting. Thus, if there are eight words on a page and a child counts to nine because she has left out "seven" in counting, she does have a concept of wordness. Note also that if the child counts words, she understands the terminology for words; some children will count the letters instead, revealing that they do not yet differentiate the meanings of "word" and "letter.")

10. Read the remainder of the book to the child, pointing to words as you read.

11. Mark the appropriate descriptors under "Book Handling" on the evaluation sheet and record comments about the child's performance.

Reading a Predictable Book

Materials:
• *I Like Hats* or another predictable book

1. For the third reading of *I Like Hats*, ask the child if he'd like to read the text to you. If the child prefers to have you read along, do so with only the amount of assistance the child requires to keep the reading fluent. Share the reading with the child but give him as much responsibility as possible. Ask the child to point to the text as he reads.

2. As the child reads, observe such things as:

   • willingness to participate.
   • degree of participation.
   • degree of voice-print match.
   • how he uses memory, pictures, and other cues to support his reading.
   • comments or questions the child has.
   • how much of the reading you must do in order to keep the child going.
   • whether there are particular sections of the text the child needed more assistance with than others.

3. Thank the child for reading the book with you. Immediately after the child leaves, mark the appropriate descriptors under "Reading a Predictable Book" on the evaluation sheet and record comments about the child's performance.

Retelling

Materials:

- "City Mouse–Country Mouse" in *City Mouse–Country Mouse*, pictures by M. Parry (Scholastic, 1970)

or

- "Split Pea Soup" in *George and Martha*, by J. Marshall (Houghton Mifflin, 1972)

or

- a book of your choice and retelling guide for selected book

1. Introduce one of the books listed above or a story of your choice to the child. If you choose a book other than those listed, be sure it is brief and has a well-formed story. Prepare a retelling guide using those in this evaluation as models.

2. Read the title and encourage the child to talk about the title, the illustration, and what the book might be about. Before you begin reading, remind the child to listen carefully because you will be asking him to retell the story.

Unaided Retelling

3. To obtain an unaided retelling, say something like, "I would like you to retell the story, [title of story], as if I had never heard it before or as if you were retelling it to a friend." Do not interrupt the child or interject any questions until he has stopped talking; even then, a ten-second silence may encourage the child to continue without any prompting. Or say something like, "I'll give you a little while to think about it" and wait ten seconds or until the child indicates that he has nothing more to say.

4. During the unaided retelling, listen very carefully to what the child says so that you do not ask questions during the aided retelling about information the child has already given. Cross out any information provided in the child's unaided retelling on the retelling guide and mark it with a U (unaided retelling).

Aided Retelling

5. Once the unaided retelling is over, conduct an aided retelling by asking about information not already related. Questions can be devised by referring to information the child has already given you, as in the following examples, which are keyed to the basic elements of a story:

    Character recall: Who else was in the story?

    Character development: What else can you tell me about ___?

    Setting: Where did _____ happen?
    When did _____ happen?
    Tell me more about [the setting that was named].

Events: What else happened in the story?
How did _____ happen?
What happened before _____?
What happened after _____?

Plot: What was [the major character's] main problem?

Theme: What do you think [the major character] learned in this story?
What do you think the author might have been trying to tell us in this story?

6. Mark the appropriate descriptors under "Retelling" on the evaluation sheet and record pertinent comments about the child's performance.

Writing

Materials:
- drawing or drawing paper
- writing paper and pencil

These procedures may be adapted easily for use with small groups of students.

1. It is almost always best to allow children to write *and* draw during a writing session. You might give the child the drawing she did as a part of the "Drawing" task and tell her to add a favorite friend to the picture. Or you can begin with a fresh sheet of paper and ask the child to draw herself doing something with a friend. Let the child know that you also want her to tell the story of the picture by writing it. As the child works, you should also draw a picture of yourself with a friend.

2. As the child begins to finish the drawing, give her the kind of paper that is (or will be) often used for writing. Tell the child that you would like her to write about her friend and/or what she and her friend do together. Tell the child that you will not help her and that whatever she does will be fine.

3. If the child has not previously written or if she is uncomfortable with writing, demonstrate the task by sharing your drawing and composing a couple of sentences about your friend on your writing paper. As you write the first sentence, think aloud about the process of spelling words as they sound, using invented spelling. As you write the second sentence, ask the child to listen as you sound out some of the words you want to use and to help decide what letters to use for those sounds.

4. Then encourage the child to write her own story about her friend. Remind her that you will not help her and that she should solve problems for herself the best she can. Again, indicate that whatever she does will be fine.

5. Record notes about the following:

   - Whether the child asks for help even though you have told her none is available.
   - The child's knowledge of sound/letter relationships (observed as you wrote your own story).
   - Whether the child shifts back and forth between drawing and writing.
   - Comments or talk during writing.
   - Rereading during writing.

   Write down anything that provides you with information about how the child approaches the task, especially with regard to fluency, or about the child's language or social development.

6. If the child still claims that she cannot write, tell her to pretend to write. Have a quick conference with the child, saying something like, "Tell me something about your friend (or what you are doing with your friend in the picture)." Listen to what the child says and then say, "Now write that down." Be careful not to ask questions that would suggest specific ideas the child might write about. If a child is only drawing and not writing, remind her that you'd like her to write now. If the child continues drawing, it may be that she doesn't know the difference between writing and drawing or does not yet feel comfortable sharing her attempts.

7. Try not to distract the child from writing by talking with her, but do talk with a child who appears to require encouragement or further information. Do *not* make comments about the child's writing (not even "You're doing a good job!"). If you do not understand something that you see or observe, ask the child a quick question about it.

8. When the child finishes, ask her to read the piece to you. Write what the child reads or pretends to read in the space provided on the evaluation sheet.

9. Respond to the *content* of the writing in a specific and positive way, e.g., "That's wonderful that you've known Betsy for such a long time" or "It sounds like you enjoyed your trip to the amusement park with Betsy." If the child starts talking more about her friend as she finishes reading the piece, stop the child and say, "Add something about what you just told me" or write on your observation sheet that the child had much more to say than she wrote down.

10. If the child refuses to write or writes a story in which she uses mostly words she knows how to spell, offer to write for the child. Ask the child what she wants to say about her friend and begin to write it. But instead of only taking a dictation, ask the child to listen to the sounds as you write each word and to help

you decide what letters to write for those sounds. For example, if the child wants to say, "Me and my friend play dolls," and you ask her to help you with "friend," write whatever the child says she hears. That could be only a letter or two; write it and go on to the next word. Use this information to help you decide what the child knows and doesn't know about sound/letter relationships. It is possible the child knows far more than she is willing or able to use when she herself writes.

11. After the child has left, review your observation notes, clarify, and add to them. Mark the appropriate descriptors under "Writing," using your observation notes and the child's writing sample.

School of Education, University of Coloraodo at Denver Instructional Assistance Project, Denver Public Schools

Emergent Reading and Writing
Evaluation Sheet

The information you gather will help you make decisions about reading and writing instruction. With that in mind, mark those descriptors that best fit the child being evaluated and make notes about anything else that will inform your instruction.

Mark as many descriptors as necessary to represent the child's behavior within each descriptor category. MARK MORE THAN ONE DESCRIPTOR WITHIN EACH CATEGORY IF MORE THAN ONE FITS THE CHILD'S BEHAVIOR. If no descriptors are appropriate within a category or if the descriptors provided do not capture some or all of the child's behavior, describe the child's behavior in "Other observations, comments, and notes."

Drawing

Independence in drawing

_____ Little.
_____ Moderate.
_____ A great deal.

Concentration/interest in drawing

_____ Little.
_____ Moderate.
_____ A great deal.

Name Writing
(done as part of "Drawing")

Concentration/interest in writing name

_____ Little.
_____ Moderate.
_____ A great deal.

Knowledge of writing first name (disregard letter directionality and formation)

_____ No knowledge of how to write first name.

_____ Minimum understanding that the name is composed of letters/symbols.

_____ Able to write one or two letters in name.

_____ Able to write several letters in name.

_____ Able to write most or all the letters in name.

Knowledge of writing last name (disregard letter directionality and formation)

_____ No knowledge of how to write last name.

_____ Minimum understanding that the name is composed of letters/symbols.

_____ Able to write one or two letters in name.

_____ Able to write several letters in name.

_____ Able to write most or all the letters in name.

Other observations, comments, and notes:

_____

_____

_____

_____

Dictation

Length and fluency of dictation

_____ Labels objects in picture only.

_____ Less than 3 thoughts or sentences.

_____ 3-6 thoughts or sentences with a lot of prompting.

_____ 3-6 thoughts or sentences with a little prompting.

_____ 3-6 thoughts or sentences with no prompting.

Pacing of dictation

_____ Too slow/labored.

_____ Too fast for you to write.

_____ Pacing is variable; child sometimes attends to the pace of your writing and other times does not.

_____ Waits for you to finish each word before dictating another word.

_____ Waits for you to finish writing phrase/sentence/thought before dictating another.

Interest in dictation

_____ No attention paid to the writing you do during dictation.

_____ Scant attention paid to the writing you do during dictation.

_____ General attention given to the writing you do during dictation (child looks at the paper but doesn't appear to focus on print).

_____ Child's attention is focused on the words that you are writing and saying.

_____ Child attempts to reread as you are writing.

Other observations, comments, and notes:

_____

_____

_____

_____

First Reading of Dictation

In the space below, write what the child reads or pretends to read for the dictation:

_____

_____

_____

_____

_____

_____

_____

Child's reliance when reading or pretending to read dictation

_____ Refused to read or to pretend read.

_____ Retold or pretended to read from memory.

_____ Read only random known words.

_____ Relied on memory and known words to read.

_____ Relied on memory, known words, and other print cues to read.

Match between dictation and reading of dictation

_____ Little match.

_____ Moderate match.

_____ High match based on reading of text; some miscues didn't make sense.

_____ High match based on reading of text; if miscues were made, they made sense.

Directionality

_____ Did not point top to bottom or left to right.

_____ Consistently pointed top to bottom *or* left to right.

_____ Consistently pointed top to bottom *and* left to right.

Voice-print match

_____ No voice print match.

_____ Sporadic voice print match.

_____ Voice print match well established.

Recognition of words and sentences

_____ Located no words.

_____ Located 1 of 3 requested words.

_____ Located 2 of 3 requested words.

_____ Located all 3 requested words.

_____ Located requested sentence.

Other observations, comments, and notes:

_____

_____

_____

_____

Name Reading
(done as part of "First Reading of Dictation")

Reading of name

_____ Unable to recognize name.

_____ Able to read first name only.

_____ Able to read first and last name.

Recognition of letters in name

_____ Named no letter correctly.

_____ Named 1 or 2 of 6 letters correctly.

_____ Named 3 or 4 of 6 letters correctly.

_____ Named 5 or 6 of 6 letters correctly.

Other observations, comments, and notes:

_____

_____

_____

_____

Second Reading of Dictation

In the space below, write what the child reads or pretends to read for the dictation:

_____

_____

_____

_____

_____

_____

Child's reliance when reading or pretending to read dictation

_____ Refused to read or to pretend read (includes "I can't remember").
_____ Retold or pretended to read from memory.
_____ Read only random known words.
_____ Relied on memory and known words to read.
_____ Relied on memory, known words, and other print cues to read.

Match between dictation and reading of dictation

_____ Little match.
_____ Moderate match.
_____ High match based primarily on memory.
_____ High match based on reading of text; some miscues didn't make sense.
_____ High match based on reading of text; if miscues were made, they made sense.

Directionality

_____ Did not point top to bottom or left to right.
_____ Consistently pointed top to bottom *or* left to right.
_____ Consistently pointed top to bottom *and* left to right.

Voice-print match

_____ No voice print match.
_____ Sporadic voice print match.
_____ Voice print match well established.

Emergent Reading and Writing

Recognition of words and sentences

_____ Located no words.
_____ Located 1 of 3 requested words.
_____ Located 2 of 3 requested words.
_____ Located all 3 requested words.
_____ Located requested sentence.

Other observations, comments, and notes:

_____

_____

_____

_____

Familiarity with Literature

Familiarity with nursery rhymes

_____ Did not recognize any nursery rhymes.
_____ Recognized title(s) but was unable to recite rhyme(s).
_____ Recited rhyme(s) with considerable assistance.
_____ Recited rhyme(s) with a little assistance at the beginning.
_____ Recited rhyme(s) with no assistance.

Familiarity with favorite stories

_____ Could not name favorite stories or story characters.
_____ Named story(ies) and/or characters but could not tell about story(ies).
_____ Named story(ies) and/or characters and told about them.

List favorite story(ies) and/or characters:

_____

_____

_____

Familiarity with traditional folk tales

_____ Was familiar with 0 folk tales.
_____ Was familiar with 1 folk tale.
_____ Was familiar with 2 folk tales.
_____ Was familiar with 3 folk tales.
_____ Was familiar with 4 folk tales.

List traditional folk tales recognized:

_____

_____

_____

Other observations, comments, and notes:

_____

_____

_____

_____

Book Handling

Title

_____ Unable to label "title" or tell its function.
_____ Able to label "title" or tell its function.

Place to begin reading

_____ Book held upside down or backwards.
_____ Book held correctly but not opened to title page or first page of text.
_____ Book opened to title page or first page of text.

Place to continue reading

_____ Pointed to picture on right-hand page (wrong page).
_____ Pointed to picture on left-hand page (right page).
_____ Pointed to some print on right-hand page (wrong page).
_____ Pointed to print other than first word on left-hand page (right page).
_____ Pointed to first word on left-hand page.

Wordness

_____ No evidence of understanding of wordness (including random counting).
_____ Counted each letter.
_____ Counted each word.

Other observations, comments, and notes:

_____
_____
_____
_____

Reading a Predictable Book

Willingness to read/pretend to read predictable book

_____ Refused to read/pretend to read.
_____ Read/pretended to read only with the teacher.
_____ Independently read/pretended to read at least part of the time.

Teacher assistance needed by child

_____ Needed assistance in all or most of the reading.
_____ Needed assistance for some of the reading.
_____ Needed minimum or no assistance.

Voice-print match

_____ No voice-print match.
_____ Sporadic voice-print match.
_____ Consistent voice-print match.

Reading cues

_____ Refused to read/pretend to read.
_____ Relied mostly on pictures and memory.
_____ Read some known words but mostly relied on pictures and memory.
_____ Relied on print features, pictures and memory to read.

Reading miscues

_____ Refused to read/pretend to read or only did so with teacher assistance.
_____ Miscues did not make sense.
_____ Miscues made sense but were not graphophonically similar to the words in the story.
_____ Miscues made sense and were graphophonically similar to the words in the story.

Other observations, comments, and notes:

_____

_____

_____

_____

Emergent Reading and Writing

Retelling

Using the retelling guide for the book that the child heard you read, cross off information that the child provides in the retelling. Leave information that the child does not mention unmarked. For example, if the child talks about the country mouse offering food to the city mouse but does not mention that it was plain food, mark the line accordingly:

~~Country mouse offers~~ plain ~~food.~~

In addition, mark "U" next to the information the child provides in the unaided retelling and "A" next to the information the child provides in the aided retelling. Thus, if the child has given the above information about the country mouse giving the city mouse food and the child tells you that the food was plain after you ask a question in the aided retelling like, "What kind of food did the country mouse offer to the city mouse?," you can mark the retelling guide for that information as follows:

A

U   ~~Country mouse offers (plain) food.~~

Use the remaining space on this page for notes about the child's retelling. The retelling guides are on the next two pages.

Story the child heard:

_____

Observations, comments, and notes about the retelling:

_____

_____

_____

_____

_____

_____

_____

_____

_____

_____

City Mouse-Country Mouse: Retelling Guide

Characters	Development
Country Mouse	Not fussy about food. Willing to share. Peaceful.
City Mouse	Fussy about food. Willing to take risks.

Setting

In the country at first; then in the city.

Events

City Mouse visits country mouse.

Country Mouse offers plain food to city mouse.

City Mouse invites country mouse to the city for a feast.

The mice go to the city.

Barking dogs charge into the dining hall.

The mice run away.

Country Mouse decides to go home where he can eat in peace.

Plot

Country Mouse and City Mouse go to the city for a feast and get chased away by dogs; Country Mouse decides to go back to the country and his plain food.

Theme

It's better to eat plain food in peace than fine food if you can't enjoy it.

Split Pea Soup: Retelling Guide

Characters	Development
Martha	Liked to make pea soup. Was a good friend to George.
George	Didn't like pea soup. Didn't want to hurt Martha's feelings.

Setting

At Martha's house

Events

Martha made lots of split pea soup.

George ate Martha's soup but hated it.

George poured the soup in his loafers so he wouldn't have to eat any more and so he wouldn't hurt Martha's feelings.

Martha saw George pour soup in his shoes.

Martha said that friends always tell each other the truth.

Martha told George he wouldn't have to eat any more soup and admitted that she didn't like it either.

George and Martha ate chocolate chip cookies instead.

Plot

George pretends to like Martha's split pea soup. When Martha discovers he doesn't like it, they eat cookies instead.

Theme

It's better to tell your friends the truth.

Writing

In the space below, write down what the child reads or pretends to read for his/her writing:

_____

_____

_____

_____

_____

_____

_____

_____

Concentration/interest in writing

_____ Little.

_____ Moderate.

_____ A great deal.

Fluency of writing

_____ Did not write.

_____ Wrote with a lot of prompting.

_____ Wrote with a little prompting.

_____ Wrote with no prompting.

Revision process

_____ Did not write.

_____ Neither reread nor revised while writing.

_____ Reread while writing.

_____ Revised handwriting or spelling during writing.

_____ Revised content during writing.

Directionality

_____ Indicated lack of knowledge of directionality.

_____ Consistently wrote top to bottom *or* left to right.

_____ Consistently wrote top to bottom *and* left to right.

Message representation

_____ Mostly random scribbles or "cursivelike" scribbles.
_____ Mostly letterlike formations.
_____ Mostly limited or repeated use of letters, numbers, and/or random known or copied words.
_____ Generally used a variety of letters and numbers.
_____ Generally used functional/invented spelling.

Use of graphophonics

_____ No apparent sound/letter relationships.
_____ Represented the sounds heard at the beginning of words.
_____ Represented the sounds heard at the beginning and end of words only.
_____ Represented a few of the sounds heard within words (more than just the beginning and end of words).
_____ Represented the majority of sounds heard in words (you can read most of what the child writes without asking the child to read it to you).

Syntax

_____ Did not write (no evidence of syntax).
_____ Labeled picture items (no evidence of syntax).
_____ Wrote connected text but did not use syntactic markers such as word boundaries and punctuation.
_____ Occasionally denoted word boundaries by using white space, dashes, "periods," or some other mark between words.
_____ Occasionally denoted thought boundaries by using periods, commas, or some other punctuation.

Message meaning and organization

_____ Indicated no message intent.
_____ Conveyed ideas (even if they weren't written down) but ideas were not related to drawing.
_____ Conveyed ideas (even if they weren't written down) and ideas were related to drawing.
_____ Organized ideas (even if they weren't written down) into a pattern that made the message clear.
_____ Written text made sense standing alone (you can read the invented spelling, the ideas are organized, and it made sense without referring to the drawing).

Reading the message

_____ Refused to read or to pretend to read.
_____ Pretended to read with no focus on print.
_____ Pretended to read while focusing on print.
_____ Read own writing with difficulty.
_____ Read own writing with relative ease.

Other observations, comments, and notes:

_____

_____

_____

_____

Emergent Reading and Writing Evaluation reprinted with permission of the authors and Denver Public Schools, Denver, Colorado.

Emergent Reading and Writing Evaluation

People Involved in Development

Lynn K. Rhodes, University of Colorado at Denver, Associate Professor

Mary Ann Bash, Denver Public Schools, Instructional Consultant, Chapter I Program

Nancy L. Shanklin, University of Colorado at Denver, Associate Professor

Wendy Downie, Denver Public Schools, Resource Specialist, Chapter I Program

Debbie Milner, Denver Public Schools, Resource Specialist, Chapter I Program

Catherine M. Felknor, Independent Evaluation Consultant

Malinda Jones, Denver Head Start Extended Day Program, Supervisor, University of Northern Colorado, Adjunct Professor

Numerous teachers in the Denver Public Schools Chapter I Program

Evaluation Instruments Referred to in Development

Clay, M. (1972, 1979). *Concepts about print test.* Portsmouth, NH: Heinemann.

Goodman, Y. M., & B. Altwerger. (1981). Pre-schoolers' book handling knowledge. In Print awareness in pre-school children: A working paper. Occasional Papers: Research Paper #4. Tucson, AZ: Program in Language and Literacy, College of Education, University of Arizona. Also in Stage 1 Teacher's Resource Manual for the *Bookshelf* Program. New York: Scholastic.

McCormick, S. (1981). Assessment and the beginning reader: Using student-dictated stories. *Reading World, 21,* 29-39.

4

Literacy at Home

The Student Interview

Gathering initial information about home literacy from children is preferable to gathering it from parents. Asking "Who reads to you at home?" of a child seems less intrusive than asking "Does someone at home read to your child?" of a parent. Because you see the children on a daily basis, it is also far easier to gather much of the initial information about home literacy at school. This information can shape the direction of ensuing conversations with parents about literacy at home.

The questions on the student interview are designed to find out several important things:

1. The nature of the home literacy environment. All homes in the United States are literate environments; your job is to discover the degree of literacy in the environment and the sources of print available to the child.

2. The nature of the literate demonstrations in the home. Are the demonstrations by others (such as ads on TV) and/or by those the child lives with? If those the child lives with provide literacy demonstrations, what sort of demonstrations are they? Who provides these demonstrations and who does not?

3. The nature of the child's engagement in literacy at home. Does someone in the home interact with the child over print? What is the nature of these interactions? What materials are used in these interactions?

Once you have collected the information, you can use it in a variety of ways. The information will be of use to you in determining the sort of literacy environment, demonstrations, and engagement you need to plan in school. For example, if some children do not have books at home it becomes even more important to plan large chunks of book reading time in school. If some children come from homes in which they have been read to for years, you may be able to build on and extend those experiences more effectively.

The information can also help you determine which children's relatives could best support literacy opportunities at home and what kind of support might be useful to them. It may be the child's older brother or grandmother who offers the child literacy opportunities; working with the person who has already revealed that he or she has the time and interest is more likely to pay off.

Name _____   Date _____

Student Interview

1. Do you read when you are at home? What kinds of things? How often? (As you are talking with the child, find out what sorts of reading materials are in the home, where they are kept, how many books the child owns, whether he or she can name titles, who owns and uses the reading materials, whether any are from the public library, etc. If the child does not talk about books, newspapers, and/or magazines, find out if the child is aware of people in the home reading print on TV ads, in the TV guide, in recipes, on food labels or posters, and so on.)

   _____

   _____

   _____

   _____

   _____

2. Who reads things to you at home? What kinds of things? How often? (The child may name people other than parents. As in the first question, probe for what is read to the child other than books if there are no books in the home. If no one reads to the child, find out who the child thinks might want to do that.)

   _____

   _____

   _____

   _____

   _____

3. Do you write when you are at home? What kinds of things? How often? What happens to these pieces of writing? (As you are talking with the child, find out what sorts of writing materials are in the home, where they are kept, what kind of access the child has to them, who owns and uses the writing materials, what sorts of things are written, etc.)

   _____

   _____

   _____

   _____

   _____

4. Who helps you write things at home? What kinds of things? How often? (The child may name people other than parents. If no one helps the child write at home, find out who the child thinks might want to help.)

_____

_____

_____

_____

_____

Other Notes:

_____

_____

_____

_____

_____

The Parent Interview

Like the student interview, the parent interview is designed to be conducted orally. If you cannot conduct an oral interview with each parent, consider the following:

- Conduct oral interviews selectively, perhaps with the parents of the children who concern you most.

- Send the interview home for a written response when you are certain that the parent(s) will respond.

- Send home only two questions per week instead of all of them at once.

- Ask only the two or three questions you find most informative. Those may vary from parent to parent and may be dependent on the information you have previously gathered from the student interview.

- Give the parents an option to complete the interview in writing at an information session or "back to school" night.

Preface the oral interview with an explanation about why you are giving the interview: that talking with parents about their children helps you to know the child better and plan instruction more effectively. All questions should serve these dual purposes. You'll notice that every question is designed to help you get to know the child better and to understand the parents' goals for the child's literacy.

Even in oral interview settings, be sensitive to parents who may not themselves be literate. For example, in an oral interview, it may not be a good idea to give the questions to the parent but rather to leave them on a clipboard on the table in front of you. One fifth-grade girl told her Chapter I teacher, "My mom won't come to conferences anymore because the teachers always stick a bunch of my papers in front of her to look at and she can't read them." Giving parents the option of filling out the interview at "back to school" night or taking it home allows those who can't read and/or write to take it home and not respond. Ask those parents to come in for an oral interview.

Let the parent know that you'll take notes during the session so that you can remember later what was said. Listen carefully to what the parent says and ask follow-up questions to clarify or to gather more information. Give the parent time to respond to a question; silences may be long for you but the parent is busy thinking and should be given time to do so.

Name _____ Date _____

Child's name _____ Grade _____

Parent Interview

1. How do you think your child is doing as a reader/writer? Why? (If a young child: What signs have you seen that your child is ready to learn to read/write?)

   _____

   _____

   _____

   _____

2. What would you like your child to do as a reader/writer that he or she isn't doing now?

   _____

   _____

   _____

   _____

3. Do you ever notice your child reading/writing at home? Tell me about it.

   _____

   _____

   _____

   _____

4. What do you think your child's attitude is toward reading/writing? What do you think has helped to create this attitude?

   _____

   _____

   _____

   _____

5. What sorts of questions about your role in helping your child become a better reader/writer might you like to ask me?

   _____

   _____

   _____

   _____

Literacy at Home

6. Since I like to help the children read and write about things they are interested in, it helps me to know each individual child's interests. What kinds of things does your child like to do in his or her free time?

_____

_____

_____

_____

7. Is there anything about the child's medical history that might affect his or her reading/writing? Is there anything else that might affect his or her reading/writing?

_____

_____

_____

_____

8. Is there anything else that you think would be helpful for me to know in teaching your child?

_____

_____

_____

_____

Parent Letter

The letter that follows was used by Roxanne Torke, a first- and second-grade teacher in the Denver Public Schools. Unlike those in the previous oral interview, the questions on this letter are designed to be answered very briefly in writing. Parents can ask their own questions and say as much as they like in response to Torke's open-ended invitation to share "anything else," or they can decide not to reply beyond the short answer portion of the letter.

Torke used the parents' responses to the letter to focus her presentation about reading at a parent get-together. At this meeting, she talked about general trends in reading progress in the class, answered the questions several parents asked, and dealt with concerns that seemed to have general relevance for all the parents. This exploration of the information provided by the parents allowed Torke to deal more completely with parent observations and concerns in a group meeting, and provided each parent with advance perspective on other children's progress and other parents' viewpoints about reading development. In addition, Torke was able to use the presentation to help parents better understand reading development and how she and they could support it together.

Individual responses to the letter also helped Torke focus the individual conference she had with each parent. Torke especially wanted to discuss changes in behavior and attitude that the parents pointed out but that Torke had not observed, changes that Torke had observed that the parents had not, and changes that the parent and Torke seemed to disagree about. In addition, the conference allowed Torke to help the parent understand, when necessary, how to create a more supportive literacy environment at home.

Dear Parents:

I'm preparing for our parent get-together next Tuesday night and for conferences Thursday and Friday. I would really appreciate your taking some time to think about your child as a reader. Have you noticed any changes over the last four months? What is your child doing differently?

Please write "yes," "no," or "some" next to the following statements that apply to your child:

My child . . .

seems more interested in reading. _____

is reading signs and other print in the environment. _____

talks about books more. _____

seems to be thinking about books on a deeper level. _____

makes connections between books and his or her life. _____

spends more time reading alone. _____

asks if someone will listen to him or her read more. _____

asks if someone will read to him or her more. _____

can sound out unknown words better. _____

uses other strategies to figure out unknown words like reading to the end of the sentence. _____

reads to a sibling. _____

seems to be adding new words to his or her vocabulary. _____

is more curious about the meaning of words. _____

is reading (or asking someone to read) a wider variety of books. _____

Your observations are very helpful to me in planning instruction for your child. Please share with me <u>anything</u> else you've noticed or your child has said that will help me better understand your child. Feel free to fill up the back of this paper!

Also, if you have any questions about your child's progress in any area, please write them down.

I'm looking forward to seeing you twice next week.

Parent Letter by Roxanne Torke. Reprinted with permission of the author.

Data Gathering: Three Perspectives

Letters to Parents
My Child as a Reader
The Child as a Reader
Me as a Reader

The assessment forms and procedures that follow were designed by Dawn Jamieson, a teacher in British Columbia, Canada, and an instructor at Okanagan College in Vernon, British Columbia.

The three forms involve the parents, the teacher, and the primary-grade child in evaluating the reading progress of the child. The parents', teacher's, and child's forms are set up so that each is asked to observe and comment on similar aspects of reading. The completed forms are designed to be compared and discussed at a parent-teacher-student conference.

Although the forms are not designed to assess literacy only at home, the parents' observations reflect the child's literacy at home. It is useful to compare these observations of the child's literacy at home with the observations the teacher makes about literacy at school and the observations the child makes about him or herself both at home and at school.

Also included in this handbook are the letters that Jamieson uses when she initially sends the forms home and when she sends the forms home again the week prior to the conference.

Similar forms, based on the same notion of gathering data from three perspectives, have been developed for intermediate students, their parents, and teachers. In addition, Jamieson's primary forms have been adapted to include both reading and writing. These forms may be found in *Evaluating Literacy* (Anthony, Johnson, Mickelson, & Preece, 1991, pgs. 42-47).

Reference

Anthony, R. J., T. D. Johnson, N. I. Mickelson, and A. Preece. (1991). Evaluating Literacy: A Perspective for Change. Portsmouth, NH: Heinemann.

Dear Parents:

Your child will be involved in an exciting adventure this year. He or she is continuing to learn to read, write, listen and speak. While the prime responsibility for this important learning rests with the child, you as parents and I as the teacher will need to be aware, alert, and supportive of the learner.

Because we are all involved in this important learning process, I have made observation guidelines for each of us. We will all be asking how the learner is doing. We will all be evaluating.

With this letter I have included my observational guidelines for parents. These guidelines focus on the types of behaviors you may see your child involved in as he or she grows and develops. You are uniquely able to see if your child is using reading, writing, listening, and speaking in everyday situations—to see how he or she is really becoming literate.

Please refer to these guidelines when you are with your child over the next three months. One week before the next reporting period, I will send another copy of the guidelines home. Before you come in for our parent/teacher interview, please take time to go through the guidelines and record your observations of your child.

At that time I will have completed a similar form and so will your child. Consideration of the completed forms will contribute to our evaluation of your child's progress toward literacy.

Sincerely,

Data Gathering: Three Perspectives by Dawn Jamieson. Reprinted with permission of the author.

Dear Parents:

It is almost time for us to meet and discuss your child's progress since the beginning of the year. I am sending you additional copies of the observation guidelines so that you can have time to consider and complete them before our conference.

Please bring them with you when you come for your parent/teacher conference.

I would also like to have your child join us. He or she will be completing his or her observation forms during school time this week.

I look forward to our meeting. It will be interesting to evaluate together your child's progress.

Sincerely,

Name _____ Date _____

Teacher _____ Grade _____

My Child as a Reader
(An Observational Guide for Parents)

With a vertical slash on the line indicate where you see your child's interest and participation in the reading process. Make comments or give examples of behaviors observed.

Never	Seldom	Sometimes	Often
(shows little interest)		(shows enthusiasm and attention)	

1. My child likes me to read to him or her. (e.g., brings books from school library to share; likes regular bedtime stories)	├────────────────┤
2. My child reads stories to me.(e.g., shares stories he or she has read at school; reads or attempts to read his or her own books and library books)	├────────────────┤
3. My child attempts to read in everyday situations. (e.g., street signs; store signs; cereal boxes, etc.)	├────────────────┤
4. My child can retell a story so that I can understand it. (e.g., retells a story heard at school; retells a story to a brother, sister, or friend)	├────────────────┤
5. My child figures out new words he or she sees. (e.g., uses letter sounds and meaning clues to read a store or street sign; perseveres in figuring out unknown words in a story)	├────────────────┤
6. When my child reads he or she "guesses" at words, but they usually make sense in the story. (e.g., the story might say "John was racing home" but child reads, "John was running home.")	├────────────────┤

Comments:

_____

_____

_____

_____

Printed with permission of Dawn Jamieson.

Name _____ Date _____

Teacher _____ Grade _____

The Child as a Reader
(An Observational Guide for Teachers)

With a vertical slash on the line indicate where you see the child's interest and participation in the reading process. Make comments or give examples of behaviors observed.

Never	Seldom	Sometimes	Often
(shows little interest)		(shows enthusiasm and attention)	

1. The child shows he or she enjoys literature by: • listening to stories. • chanting stories and poems. • reading to him or herself. • reading "favorites" to others. • completing reading patterns.	├────────────────┤
2. The child shows an understanding of written language by: • retelling stories (summarizing). • asking questions (clarifying). • suggesting completions and outcomes (predicting). • making pictures to illustrate stories. • following written directions. • reading with "expression."	├────────────────┤
3. The child shows efficient use of multiple cueing systems: • semantic (uses meaning cues and strategies such as rereading and reading ahead; checking titles and illustrations). • syntactic ("guesses" word that fits; observes punctuation; interchanges "a, an, the" suitably). • graphophonic (knows letter sounds; tries various letter combinations and sounds along with other clues to figure out "hard" words).	├────────────────┤

Comments:

This child's reading strengths are . . .

_____

Areas in this child's reading that I need to give special attention to are . . .

_____

Printed with permission of Dawn Jamieson.

Literacy at Home

Name _____   Date _____

Teacher _____   Grade _____

Me as a Reader
(An Observational Guide for Young Readers)

Please make a face to show how you feel about the following sentences about reading.

If you feel this way <u>often</u> make: 😊

If you feel this way <u>sometimes</u> make: 🙂

If you <u>seldom</u> feel this way make: 😐

If you <u>never</u> feel this way make: ☹️

1. I like to read. (Reading is fun; I get books from the library.)	
2. I like other people to read stories to me. (I take books home from school; I ask my parents to buy books and read to me.)	
3. I can read by myself and when I hit a hard word I try to figure it out by saying the sounds together.	
4. When I don't know a word I sometimes just guess and put in a word that sounds all right and makes sense.	
5. When I come to a period I know what to do. (I stop, take a breath, make my voice go down.)	
6. If I could pick, I would mostly read books about . . . _____	

Comments:

The best thing about reading is . . .

_____

_____

The worst thing about reading is . . .

_____

_____

Printed with permission of Dawn Jamieson.

5

Program Placement

Program Placement

The rating scales that follow were used in Denver Public School's kindergarten and elementary Chapter I programs for several reasons:

1. To determine which children most needed Chapter I instructional assistance.

    The teacher judgments were used in conjunction with the reading comprehension score from a norm-referenced test to assist Chapter I teachers in selecting students for the Chapter I program.

2. To encourage teachers to assess important aspects of reading and writing.

    What is assessed becomes important to teachers and affects what they decide to do instructionally. For example, the first time these rating scales were used, many teachers began to consider using writing activities and retellings in their classrooms.

3. To encourage Chapter I and classroom teachers to communicate with each other about children's progress in each of the areas on the rating scale.

    Although most classroom teachers were using basals (the reason for the wording on the scales) while the Chapter I teachers used literature, establishing a common language about reading and writing enabled them to communicate about children's progress more effectively.

4. To identify for classroom teachers the nature and philosophy of the instructional support students would receive from Chapter I teachers.

    Many classroom teachers expected that the Chapter I program would provide isolated skills instruction as it had in the past. The change in philosophy could be communicated, in part, by the change in assessment criteria for eligibility.

The timeline and procedures for using the rating scales for program placements were as follows:

1. Classroom teachers filled out the grid on each student in the spring of the school year.

2. The data were turned into the district Chapter I office and calculations were made to determine the lowest scoring children on the rating scale. These were potential Chapter I students for the following school year.

3. When school began, the norm-referenced test scores were checked for each child who was identified as a potential Chapter I student the previous spring. If the norm-referenced test score was under 30 percent, the child was eligible for Chapter I.

4. Since numerous children move over the summer, other indicators (such as previous enrollment in Chapter I and/or test scores) were consulted in order to make program placements for these children in the fall. In addition, classroom teachers used the rating scale on children new to the school after the new students had been in school long enough to make judgments about them.

Classroom Teacher Judgment Rating Scale

Directions: To aid in accurately identifying pupils in most need of supplemental reading instruction provided by Chapter I, you are asked to rate each pupil in your class as a 5(in B only), 4, 3, 2, or 1 on each of the following criteria:

A. Basal level performance

    4. Above grade level.

    3. Approximately at grade level.

    2. 1/2 to 1 1/2 years below grade level.

    1. More than 1 1/2 years below grade level.

B. Comprehension of written material in present basal placement (listening to stories for first graders).

    5. Can retell narrative material (character, setting, plot) and can locate major details in factual texts.

    4. Can retell only narrative material.

    3. Can retell the broad sense of text but lacks continuity or detail.

    2. Can retell only fragments of text.

    1. Cannot retell.

C. Makes sense when reading orally

    4. Corrects errors that interrupt meaning on own initiative.

    3. Reads words that could make sense.

    2. Substitutes words that don't make sense.

    1. Doesn't attempt to deal with unknown words (omits or asks for help).

D. Attitude toward reading

    4. Chooses to read frequently in leisure time on own initiative.

    3. Chooses to read occasionally on own initiative.

    2. Reads reluctantly at adult suggestion.

    1. Avoids reading.

E. Writing process

    4. Drafts, revises, elaborates, edits, and shares own writing.

    3. Rereads while writing to make a few content or organizational changes between drafts.

    2. Makes few if any changes. Changes made are to handwriting or spelling. May write very little.

    1. Does not risk writing own ideas. May copy print from classroom.

F. Writing product

    4. Displays clearly organized thoughts written with voice and literary techniques and uses conventions at or above grade level.

    3. Organizes and develops thought to make message clear but does not use conventions appropriate to grade level; or unorganized message with grade-level conventions.

    2. Produces ideas that are not well-developed or cohesive or don't make sense and uses few conventions appropriate for grade level.

    1. Produces little or no writing. If the child produces writing, it does not convey a message on its own.

Kindergarten Teacher Judgment Rating Scale

Directions: To aid in accurately identifying pupils in most need of supplemental reading instruction provided by Chapter I, you are asked to rate each pupil in your class as a 4, 3, 2, or 1 on each of the following reading criteria.

A. Basal level performance

    4. Above grade level.

    3. Approximately at grade level.

    2. Below grade level expectations (for example, knows sounds for only 6 to 8 high usage letters).

    1. Severely below grade level expectations (no sound/symbol knowledge, can't copy letters, etc.).

B. Comprehension of story read aloud by adult

    4. Can retell story (characters, setting, sequence of events).

    3. Can retell the story but it lacks continuity or detail.

    2. Can retell only fragments of the story.

    1. Cannot retell.

C. Knowledge of print features

    4. Is able to "read" whole text independently after hearing it read only once.

    3. Is able to "read" whole text independently after hearing it read repeatedly.

    2. Is able to "read" familiar whole text only if reading along with adult.

    1. Is unable to read along with adult as familiar text is read.

D. Attitude toward reading

    4. Chooses to look at books frequently in leisure time on own initiative; enjoys listening to stories.

    3. Chooses to look at books occasionally on own initiative; enjoys listening to stories.

    2. Attends well during story reading but does not choose to look at books on own initiative.

    1. Does not attend well during story reading.

E. Writing process

    4. Independently contributes ideas to group-dictated work and initiates own writing (messages, signs, copying).

    3. If asked, can contribute to group-dictated work and will attempt to use symbols to communicate a written message.

    2. Beginning to differentiate writing from drawing; understands that writing communicates a message.

    1. Seems unaware that writing communicates.

F. Writing product

    4. Uses sound/letter relationships to represent ideas and focuses on the print to "read" back what he or she has written.

    3. Creates a text of scribbles, letters, and/or numbers and conveys a message when asked to "read" what he or she has written.

    2. Has difficulty attempting symbols and does not convey a message when asked to "read" own written symbols.

    1. Does not attempt to write messages.

6

Assessing the
Teaching of Literacy

Assessing the Teaching of Literacy

Just as teachers use assessment of students' literacy to inform their decisions about what to help children work on next, they can assess their own teaching to inform their decisions about what to work on next in their instruction.

The instruments included in this section were designed to help teachers reflect on their adoption of instructional practices congruent with a whole language philosophy. The instruments can be used by a teacher as a self-assessment or by others who observe teachers.

In the case of self-assessment, a teacher can use one of the instruments to reflect back on a particular lesson or a series of lessons. The instruments are also useful as a way for a teacher to review a lesson on videotape.

The first two instruments include many more elements than will take place in a single lesson. They are intended only as observational guides. The goal is not to have all the questions answered as "yes"; the goal is to have the teacher consider including as many elements as are appropriate in his or her lesson.

The instruments may also be used by others—such as fellow teachers, program supervisors, or principals—to observe teachers. Observation is most useful when it includes three steps: a conference prior to the observation, the actual observation during instruction and the recording of information by the observer, and a postobservation conference.

During the preobservation conference, the observer and teacher discuss the nature of the lesson and what focus the observation should take. Having the teacher establish the focus of the observation assumes that teachers are most ready for information about what they have identified as particular focuses for them. The first and second instruments included here can be used during the preconference to consider the upcoming lesson with the listed elements in mind; are there other elements that are appropriate to include in the lesson?

The postconference consists of a conversation that initially addresses the focus the teacher identified in the preconference. If useful to the teacher, the conference can also attend to other concerns. Of course, it is just as important to discuss strengths as it is to discuss areas the teacher believes need attention. An observer who specifically describes a teacher's strengths can build a teacher's confidence and willingness to take risks. Together the observer and teacher can plan ways to utilize strengths in working on other areas the teacher is concerned about.

IAP Observation Checklist

This checklist was designed by Lynn Rhodes, Nancy Shanklin, and Debbie Milner to observe Chapter I (the Instructional Assistance Project) teachers in the Denver Public Schools. Through regularly scheduled in-services over a four-year period, the Chapter I teachers became familiar with whole language philosophy and instructional practices. The checklist directly reflects what had been presented and discussed during in-services. In addition to providing feedback to the teachers, the information recorded on the checklists during observations was used to plan upcoming in-services to meet the teachers' needs and address their concerns.

Observation Guide

This observation guide was developed by MaryEllen Vogt (1991) for use by supervisors and administrators working with teachers who were making changes in the literacy instruction in their classrooms. The guide served to acquaint teachers with elements found in integrated reading/language arts programs and helped supervisors and administrators to consider what could be focused on during observations. Though Vogt does not talk about using the guide for self-assessment purposes, teachers can also use the guide to help them assess their own teaching.

Coaching Form

The *Coaching Form* was developed by Nancy Shanklin for use in the master's degree practicums at the University of Colorado at Denver. The form can be open-ended because the professors and teachers develop a common philosophy, language, and expectations in university classes. In other words, the elements that make up the previous two instruments are in everyone's heads. Because teachers do practicums in their own classrooms, the observation situations differ one from another; the open-ended nature of the instrument suits any teaching situation.

Recently, the *Coaching Form* has been used by teachers in the university program prior to the practicum. Teachers take half-day professional leaves and use the form to focus observations in each other's classrooms. When teachers are unable to actually visit each other's classrooms, they have successfully used the *Coaching Form* to review videotapes of their teaching which they provide to each other.

Each of the four questions on the *Coaching Form* has a particular purpose. Because the first section, *Observations of students' responses*, is focused on students, it is often a forum for honest, nonthreatening discussions between teacher and observer about instructional ideas for meeting students' needs. The second section, *Pluses about this lesson*, affirms that teachers reflect on and improve their teaching by hearing about what they do well. The third section, *Remaining questions about this lesson*, provides a vehicle for teacher and observer to share information and solve problems.

This section makes the assumption that understanding a teacher's reasons for doing what he or she did in the lesson is critical to reflecting on what was done. The final section, *Wishes or suggestions,* gives the observer the opportunity to suggest other options the teacher might want to consider or for the observer (when the observer is a teacher) to ask the teacher for assistance that the teacher seems able to give.

When filling out the *Coaching Form,* the four sections are not meant to be completed in the order they appear. Instead, responses are recorded as they occur to the observer during the lesson.

References

Vogt, M. (1991). An observation guide for supervisors and administrators: Moving toward integrated reading/language arts instruction. *Reading Teacher, 45* (3), 206–211.

Teacher _____   Date _____

School _____   Observer _____

IAP Observation Checklist

		YES	COMMENTS
1.	The children are reading and/or writing *whole*, meaningful text representing many forms and functions.	☐	
2.	The lesson is helping children to understand that reading and writing are:		
	pleasurable.	☐	
	meaningful and relevant.	☐	
	purposeful (authentic).	☐	
3.	The print is easily observable by all of the children, and the children spend time looking at print.	☐	
4.	Reading comprehension is addressed as an evolving process with activities geared to:		
	prereading.	☐	
	during reading.	☐	
	postreading.	☐	
5.	Writing is addressed as an evolving process with time given to:		
	rehearsing.	☐	
	drafting.	☐	
	conferring and revising.	☐	
	editing.	☐	
	publishing and sharing.	☐	
6.	Children are encouraged/allowed to be independent problem solvers as they read and write.	☐	
7.	The lesson includes open-ended activities and questions that provide:		
	opportunities for reading and writing.	☐	
	sharing and extending of reading and writing.	☐	
	strategy lessons for reading and writing.	☐	
8.	Children's work is displayed in room and is kept in reading and writing folders.	☐	
9.	There is a balance between teacher-initiated and child-initiated activities.	☐	
10.	The lesson is developmentally appropriate and promotes Educational Plan objectives for each student in the group.	☐	

IAP Observation Checklist, page 2

Children's names:

_____

_____

_____

_____

_____

Brief description of the lesson:

_____

_____

_____

_____

_____

_____

Coaching notes:

_____

_____

_____

_____

_____

_____

_____

_____

_____

Amount of time observed:

_____

Amount of time children spent reading/writing:

_____

IAP Observation Checklist by Lynn K. Rhodes, Nancy L. Shanklin, and Debbie Milner. Reprinted with permission of Denver Public Schools, Denver, Colorado.

Observation Guide

Observation guide used to develop an integrated reading/language arts program

Reading

In this classroom, is the teacher:

- modeling and sharing his/her own joy of reading?
- recommending books of interest to students?
- providing a variety of literature genres (e.g., short stories, novels, poetry, biographies, essays, informational books, magazines, etc.)?
- providing time for daily, self-selected silent reading?
- reading aloud to students on a daily basis?
- requiring a minimum of oral reading practice by the students (and providing silent practice before any oral reading)?
- incorporating thematic units in language arts instruction?
- providing skills (e.g., phonics) instruction for those needing it, not in isolation but within meaningful contexts?
- utilizing a variety of grouping strategies for instruction (e.g., whole class, flexible small groups, partners, cooperative learning groups)?
- providing opportunities for students to read independently and work individually on some tasks?
- utilizing strategies that promote discussion, divergent thinking, and multiple responses?
- assigning reading tasks that promote collaboration and cooperation among students?
- planning reading tasks and strategies that activate and utilize students' prior knowledge before, during, and after reading?
- asking questions that encourage and promote dialogue, inquiry, and critique?
- encouraging a variety of responses to literature and to questions that are asked about the literature?
- collecting portfolio assessment data that is authentic in nature (e.g., transcribed, taped, or analyzed retelling) and selected for inclusion by the student and teacher so that the student, parents, and teacher all are involved in assessing progress?
- using portfolio data to guide instructional decisions and individual instruction?

Writing

In this classroom, is the teacher:

- modeling and sharing his/her joy in writing?
- modeling and teaching the stages of the writing process (prewriting, drafting, sharing, revising, editing, publishing)?
- assigning daily writing for a variety of purposes to a variety of audiences?
- encouraging divergent, creative thinking through writing assignments?
- encouraging students to use their writing as a natural response to literature?
- incorporating invented ("temporary") spelling strategies for beginning readers/writers?
- encouraging more mature writers to attempt invented spellings when composing, then assisting them with checking for correct spellings during editing?
- regularly conferring with each student about his/her writing?
- responding to student writing with helpful suggestions, thoughtful comments, and very little "red-marking"?
- promoting student self-assessment and peer conferences for the revision and editing stages?
- displaying and publishing student writing?
- collecting portfolio assessment data that is authentic in nature (e.g., samples of writing in various stages and journal entries) and selected for inclusion by the student and teacher so that the student, parents, and teacher all are involved in assessing progress?
- using portfolio data to guide instructional decisions and individual instruction?

Listening

In this classroom, is the teacher:

- promoting listening as a means of learning?
- providing opportunities for students to hear other students' responses to the literature they have read?
- providing a variety of listening experiences for differing purposes (e.g., "sharing" time, reports, Readers Theatre, students' rehearsed oral reading, etc.)?
- reading aloud to students from narrative and expository texts and from poetry selections?
- providing discussion opportunities for students to collaborate, cooperate, and compromise?
- promoting social skills through listening (e.g., providing and maintaining eye contact, paraphrasing to demonstrate understanding, and summarizing what was heard)?

Speaking

In this classroom, is the teacher:
- providing daily opportunities for structured oral language development (e.g., choral reading, speeches, drama, "sharing" time, oral reports, debates, discussion)?
- modeling and teaching correct language usage?
- teaching students to facilitate group discussion?
- modeling and teaching language for a variety of purposes (e.g., informing, persuading, sharing feelings, evaluating, imagining, predicting)?
- using literature and student writing as a source for oral language development?

General

In this classroom, is the teacher:
- actively observing and noting or recording students' responses and participation during reading/language arts instruction?
- enabling all children to make choices about what they read and write?
- resisting labeling students in terms of ability or achievement?
- communicating to parents the tenets of integrated reading/language arts instruction?
- encouraging parents to read to their children, discuss literature with them, and support and encourage their children's reading and writing progress?
- providing a structured reading environment where opinion, creative thought, and sharing of ideas are valued?
- celebrating literacy and learning on a daily basis?
- participating in staff development and then attempting to implement newly learned ideas?

Observation Guide from "An observation guide for supervisors and administrators: moving toward integrated reading/language arts instruction" by Mary Ellen Vogt. In The Reading Teacher, November 1991. Reprinted with permission of Mary Ellen Vogt and the International Reading Association.

Teacher _____

Date _____ Coach _____

Agreed Upon Focus _____

Coaching Form

Observations of students' responses to the lesson as readers and writers:

_____

_____

_____

_____

Pluses about this lesson are:

_____

_____

_____

_____

_____

_____

Remaining questions about this lesson are:

_____

_____

_____

_____

Wishes or suggestions about this lesson are:

_____

_____

_____

_____

Coaching Form by Nancy L. Shanklin. Reprinted with permission of the author.

Assessing the Teaching of Literacy

7

The Assessment and Evaluation of Literacy

The Assessment and Evaluation of Literacy

Recommended Books

Anthony, R. J., T. D. Johnson, N. I. Mickelson, A. Preece. 1991. *Evaluating literacy: A perspective for change.* Portsmouth, NH: Heinemann.

Applebee, A., J. Langer, & I. Mullis. 1989. *Understanding direct writing assessments: Reflections on a South Carolina writing study.* Princeton, NJ: Educational Testing Service.

Baskwill, J., & P. Whitman. 1988. *Whole language, whole child.* New York: Scholastic.

Belanoff, P., & M. Dickson. 1991. *Portfolios: Process and product.* Portsmouth, NH: Heinemann.

Brown, H., & B. Cambourne. 1987. *Read and retell.* Portsmouth, NH: Heinemann.

Clay, M. 1985. *The early detection of reading difficulties.* Portsmouth, NH: Heinemann.

Cohen, A. 1988. *TESTS: Marked for life?* Richmond Hill, Ontario: Scholastic-TAB.

Daly, E. (Ed.). 1990. *Monitoring children's language development: Holistic assessment in classrooms.* Portsmouth, NH: Heinemann.

Farr, R., & R. F. Carey 1986. *Reading: What can be measured?* Newark, DE: International Reading Association.

Gawith, G. 1987. *Information alive: Information skills for research and reading.* Auckland, New Zealand: Longman Paul.

Glazer, S. M., L. W. Searfoss & L. M. Gentile (Eds.). 1988. *Reexamining reading diagnosis: New trends and procedures.* Newark, DE: International Reading Association.

Goodman, K. S., Y. S. Goodman & W. J. Hood (Eds.). 1989. *The whole language evaluation book.* Portsmouth, NH: Heinemann.

Goodman, K. S., L. Bird & Y. Goodman. 1992. *The whole language catalog supplement on authentic assessment.* Santa Rosa, CA: American School Publishers.

Harp, B. (Ed.). 1991. *Assessment and evaluation in whole language programs.* Norwood, MA: Christopher Gordon.

Jett-Simpson, M. J. 1990. *Toward an ecological assessment of reading progress.* Schofield, WI: Wisconsin State Reading Association.

Johnston, P. 1992. *Constructive evaluation of literate activity.* White Plains, NY: Longman.

Kamii, C. (Ed.) 1990. *Achievement testing in the early grades: The games grown-ups play.* Washington, DC: National Association for the Education of Young Children.

Meyers, M. 1980. *A procedure for writing assessment and holistic scoring.* Urbana, IL: ERIC Clearinghouse on Reading and Communication Skills and the National Council of Teachers of English.

Morrow, L. M., & J. K. Smith (Eds.). 1990. *Assessment for instruction in early literacy.* Englewood Cliffs, NJ: Prentice Hall.

Rhodes, L. K. and N. L. Shanklin. 1993. *Windows into Literacy: Assessing Learners K-8.* Portsmouth, NH: Heinemann.

Roderick, J. (Ed.). 1991. *Context-responsive approaches to assessing children's language.* Urbana, IL: National Council of Teachers of English.

Teirney, R. J. 1991. *Portfolio assessment in the reading-writing classroom.* Norwood, MA: Christopher Gordon.

See the section on *Spelling Analysis* (pp. 84-91) for books about the assessment and evaluation of spelling.

Recommended Instruments

(There are also many instruments included in the list of recommended books.)

Barrs, M., S. Ellis, H. Heste, A. Thomas. 1988. *The primary language record.* Portsmouth, NH: Heinemann, 1989.

Clay, M. 1972, 1979. *Concepts about print test.* Portsmouth, NH: Heinemann.

Goodman, Y. M., & B. Altwerger. 1981. Pre-schoolers' book handling knowledge. In Print awareness in pre-school children: A working paper. Occasional Papers: Research Paper #4. Tucson, AZ: Program in Language and Literacy, College of Education, University of Arizona. Also in Stage 1 Teacher's Resource Manual for the *Bookshelf* Program. New York: Scholastic.

Goodman, Y. M., D. J. Watson, & C. L. Burke. 1987. *Reading miscue inventory: Alternative procedures.*

Leslie, L., & J. Caldwell. 1990. *Qualitative reading inventory.* Glenview, IL: Scott, Foresman/ Little, Brown Higher Education.

School Programs Division of the Victorian Ministry of Education. (1990). *Literacy profiles handbook: Assessing and reporting literacy development.* Brewster, NY: Touchstone Applied Science Associates (TASA).

Sharp, Q. Q. 1989. *Evaluation: Whole language checklists for evaluating your children.* New York: Scholastic.

ALSO AVAILABLE FROM HEINEMANN

Windows into Literacy
Assessing Learners K-8

Lynn K. Rhodes and Nancy Shanklin

The ideal companion to *Literacy Assessment, Windows into Literacy* suggests concrete ways for teachers and administrators to use, adapt, and invent alternate literacy assessment procedures. The majority of the book centers on the assessment of various aspects of students' reading and writing, including:

- students' metacognition
- attitudes and interests about reading and writing
- language systems and strategies used in the reading and writing process
- students' comprehension and composition
- emergent reading and writing abilities
- and much more . . .

The chapters on assessment procedures and techniques culminate in a chapter on literacy collections, including portfolios—viewed as ways to organize assessment data to present a broad-based, substantive, and coherent picture of a student's reading and writing.

Windows into Literacy will have particular value as the main text in university courses on literacy assessment and evaluation. Working teachers at the elementary and middle school level, teacher study groups, and administrators will also find this book a comprehensive, indispensable resource.

Contents: Preface. Acknowledgments. 1. Reflecting on literacy assessment 2. Literacy environments and instruction 3. Metacognitive aspects of literacy 4. Language systems and strategies in reading 5. Reading comprehension 6. Writing processe4s and products 7. Emergent reading and writing 8. Understanding and challenging traditional forms of literacy 9. Literacy collections 10. Fostering change in literacy assessment and instruction